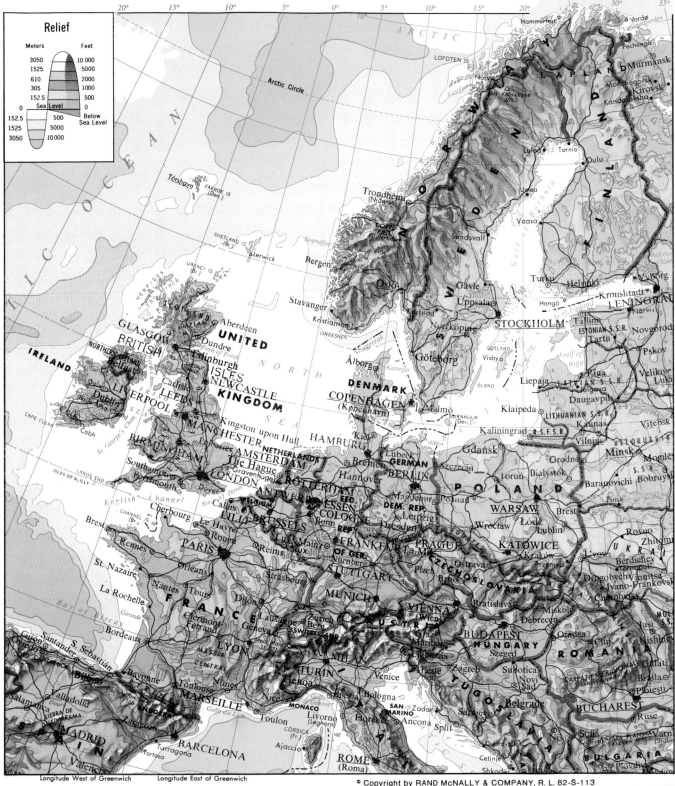

Scale 1: 16 000 000; one inch to 250 miles. Conic Projection

Elevations and depressions are given in feet

Relief

Meters		Feet
3050		10 000
1525		5000
610		2000
305		1000
152.5		500
	Sea Level	0
0	Sea Level	0 Below
152.5		500 Sea Level
1525		5000
3050		10 000

Longitude West of Greenwich   Longitude East of Greenwich

| 0 | 50 | 100 | 200 | 300 | 400 | 500 Miles |

| 0 | 100 | 200 | 400 | 600 | 800 Kilometers |

 NORTH SEA

DOGGER
BANK
60—120 Ft.

DENMARK

Thisted
Nykøbing
Skive
Struer
Holstebro
Viborg
Randers
Grenå
Ringkøbing
Herning
Silkeborg
Skanderborg
Århus
SAMSØ
Ringkøbing Fjord
Horsens
Vejle
Kalundborg
COPENHAGEN
Varde
Fredericia
Middelfart
Bogense
SJAELLAND
Ringsted
Esbjerg
Kolding
Assens
Odense
Nyborg
Korsør
Slagelse
Ribe
Haderslev
FYN
Svendborg
Vordingborg
Åbenrå
Faaborg
Rudkøbing
Maribo
Naksnov
Tønder
Sønderborg
ALS
AERØ
LANGELAND
LOLLAND
SYLT
Flensburg
FEHMARN
FÖHR
SCHLESWIG
Husum
Schleswig
Kiel Bay
HELGOLAND
Heide
Rendsburg
Eckernförde
Kiel
Neustadt
Holstein
Lübecker Bucht
Tønning
Itzehoe
Bad Oldesloe
Lübeck
HOLSTEIN
Neumünster
Elmshorn
Cuxhaven
Stade
HAMBURG
Schwerin
MECK
Bremerhaven
Lüneburg
Ludwigs
FRISIAN IS.
Norden
Wilhelmshaven
Bremen
LÜNEBURGER
ISLANDS
NORDERNEY
LANGEOOG
JUIST
BORKUM
Wesel
Weser
Emden
Oldenburg
Verden
HEIDE
Soltau
Uelzen
Delfzijl
Meer
Papenburg
Delmenhorst
NIEDERSACHSEN
FED.
REP.
OF
Celle
Groningen
Nienburg
FRISIAN
TERSCHELLING
AMELAND
Leeuwarden
Assen
Meppen
Lingen
Minden
GERMANY
Hannover
Braunschw
VLIELAND
Harlingen
Emmen
Nordhorn
TEXEL
Waddenzee
Rheine
Osnabrück
Herford
Hameln
Hildesheim
Wolfenbüttel
Den Helder
IJsselmeer
Meppel
Zwolle
Almelo
Bielefeld
Detmold
Einbeck
Blankenburg
Alkmaar
NETHERLANDS
Zaandam
Hengelo
Enschede
Gronau
Münster
Ahlen
Gütersloh
Paderborn
Northeim
Goslar
Haarlem
AMSTERDAM
Apeldoorn
Deventer
Herford
Göttingen
Leiden
Utrecht
Arnhem
Hamm
Lippstadt
Soest
Kassel
Nordhausen
The Hague
('s-Gravenhage)
Delft
Kleve
Wesel
Dortmund
Arnsberg
Eschwege
THÜ
Vlaardingen
Dordrecht
Nijmegen
Iserlohn
Mühlhausen
ROTTERDAM
Bergen
op Zoom
Breda
's-Hertogenbosch
Oberhausen
ESSEN
Hagen
Lüdenscheid
Bad Hersfeld
Vlissingen
Tilburg
Helmond
Duisburg
Mönchengl.
Wuppertal
Siegen
Gummersbach
DÜSSELDORF
Solingen
Marburg an
der Lahn
Giessen
Fulda
Hildburghsn.
Turnhout
Weert
Eindhoven
COLOGNE
(Köln)
Meiningen
Oostende
Gent
ANTWERP
Mechelen
Heerlen
Maastricht
Aachen
Düren
Bonn
Neuwied
Limburg an
der Lahn
Bad Hom
Brugge
Roeselare
Leuven
Herstal
Liège
Verviers
Eupen
Siegburg
Ahrweiler
FRANKFURT
AM MAIN
Torhout
Aalst
BRUSSELS
Nivelles
Seraing
Spa
Malmédy
Andernach
Bad Homburg
Hanau
Offenbach
Kortrijk
Tourcoing
Lille
Roubaix
BELGIUM
Namur
Dinant
RHEINLAND
Koblenz
Mainz
Darmstadt
Schwei
Armentières
Mons
Charleroi
ARDENNES
EIFEL
PFALZ
Bingen
Würzburg
Douai
Denain
Fourmies
LUX.
Bastogne
Wittlich
Kirn
Bad
Kreuznach
Aschaffenburg
FRANCE
Maubeuge
Cambrai
Givet
Wiesbaden
Maln
Cologne

Great
Yarmouth
Lowestoft
Norwich
Thetford
Bury
Edmunds
Ipswich
Harwich
Waveney
's Lynn
Chelmsford
Southend-
on-Sea
Thames
Margate
NORTH FORELAND
Ramsgate
Gillingham
Canterbury
Maidstone
Dover
N S
Folkestone
Strait of Dover
Oostende
Dunkerque
Calais
Hastings
Boulogne-
sur-Mer
Eastbourne
Étaples
CHANNEL
St. Omer
Bruges
Ieper
Béthune
Arras
Somme
St. Valéry-
sur-Somme
Le Tréport
Abbeville

Longitude East of Greenwich

© Copyright by RAND McNALLY & COMPANY, R. L. 82-S-113

0 10 20 30 40 50 60 70 80 90 100 110 120 Miles
0 20 40 60 80 100 120 140 160 180 200 Kilometers

Enchantment of the World

THE NETHERLANDS

By Dennis B. Fradin

Consultants
Wilhelmina Prins—Koeller, Press and Cultural Affairs
Consulate General of the Netherlands, Chicago, Illinois

Robert D. Haslach, Assistant to the Counselor for
Press and Cultural Affairs, Royal Netherlands Embassy, Washington, D.C.

Consultant for Social Studies; Donald W. Nylin, Ph.D., Assistant
Superintendent for Instruction, Aurora West Public Schools, Aurora, Illinois

Consultant for Reading; Robert L. Hillerich, Ph.D., Bowling Green State
University, Bowling Green, Ohio

CHILDRENS PRESS, CHICAGO

*In Spakenburg Harbor a seaman mends his equipment
while two young Nederlanders watch*

For Arthur A. Woloshin

Library of Congress Cataloging in Publication Data

Fradin, Dennis B.
  The Netherlands.

  (Enchantment of the world).
  Includes indexes.
  Summary: Discusses the history and culture of
a country in which nearly half the land is below sea
level, protected from flooding only by a network of
man-made dikes and dams.
  1. Netherlands—Juvenile literature.
[1. Netherlands] I. Title. II. Series.
DJ18.F7   1983   949.2   82-17896
ISBN-0-516-02779-4   AACR2

Picture Acknowledgments:
Courtesy Flag Research Center, Winchester,
Massachusetts 01890—Flag on back cover.
Colour Library International: 4, 16, 23 (top), 25, 26, 42, 50,
52, 53 (2 photos), 54, 56 (bottom), 57 (3 photos), 59, 61, 63,
66 (2 photos), 67 (3 photos), 70, 74, 77, 78, 79 (left), 80
(right), 84, 88 (2 photos), 102, 106, 113
The Royal Netherlands Embassy, Washington, D.C.:
Pages 8, 9, 12, 17, 22, 24, 44, 47, 55, 56 (top), 60, 62, 68, 71,
73, 85, 87, 104 (right)
Carol Barrington: 48, 79 (right), 89, 92
KLM Royal Dutch Airlines: 5, 28 (2 photos)
Jane P. Downton: 21
Greg Fox/Atoz Images: 6
Irene E. Hubbell: 18, 58
Historical Pictures Service, Chicago: 11, 30, 31, 33
(2 photos), 35, 36, 37 (2 photos), 94, 96, 97, 99 (2 photos),
100, 101, 104 (left)
Hillstrom Stock Photos: © W. S. Nawrocki, 15, 23
(bottom), 80 (left)
Len Meents, maps: 21, 38, 56, 58, 60, 65

Young girl wears the traditional headdress of Volendam in The Netherlands.

TABLE OF CONTENTS

Chapter 1

THE DUTCH BUILT
THE NETHERLANDS

On the night of January 31, 1953, a storm raged over the North Sea. The wind, howling at speeds up to 100 miles (161 kilometers) per hour, tossed ships about like bathtub toys. Titanic waves crashed toward the shore.

The Netherlands, lying alongside the North Sea in northwestern Europe, was the nation most threatened by this storm. Almost half The Netherlands lies below the level of the sea. A network of seawalls, called dikes, protects the land from the North Sea. Built over hundreds of years, the dikes have withstood all but the fiercest storms.

Whenever floods have threatened The Netherlands, the country's people (called Nederlanders, or the Dutch) have worked together to hold back the water. On that winter night in 1953 church bells tolled and sirens blasted to signal danger. By the thousands, villagers ran out to the dikes. They piled up sandbags to strengthen the dikes in places where they were about to give way.

*Aerial photograph shows the flooded town of Nieuwerkerk. Inhabited since 1233
at least, this town has frequently been threatened by storms from the sea.*

Nowhere was the spirit of cooperation stronger than in the
village of Colijnsplaat. There the sea crashed through a dike,
leaving a large open space. The townspeople piled up boards and
sandbags to block the opening. Suddenly it seemed that a pillar
would give way and the whole dike would crumble. Linking their
arms, dozens of persons went out and braced up the dike with
their own bodies. Luck then came to their aid. Waves tossed a
100-foot (30-meter) ship into the gap in the dike, blocking the sea.

Other towns weren't as lucky. Waves smashed through the
dikes in many locations, letting the sea flow into the little country.
In dozens of towns people were washed out of their homes and
drowned. Some were able to climb into trees and attics. Other
people made their way onto rooftops. There they remained while
a 12-foot (4-meter) wall of water ravaged the coast.

Water rushes through a broken dike near Terneuzen flooding the polders.

As news of the disaster spread, the government of The Netherlands sent out army and navy rescue teams. Fishermen searched the coastline for survivors. In the hours after the flood, other countries sent helicopters and boats to help rescue people from trees, rooftops, and floating wreckage.

As Operation Rescue continued, officials counted the dead. Approximately 1,800 persons had drowned. More than 50,000 cattle and other farm animals were dead. Nearly 50,000 homes were underwater and more than 130 towns were at least partly wrecked. Massive damage had been done to factories, farms, and orchards.

The broken dikes were the Nederlanders' biggest worry. In sixty-seven places the sea had smashed large holes right through them. In addition, hundreds of miles of seawalls had suffered minor damage. Before the dead were buried—even before the last rescues were made—the Dutch began to repair their broken dikes.

For more than a thousand years they have made such repairs after big storms. Every Nederlander knows the importance of the dikes. Without them, nearly half the country would be sea instead of land. The story of how the Dutch built the dikes to convert sea into land is unique in world history.

The first permanent settlers came to The Netherlands at least six thousand years ago. The land looked much different than it does today. The western part of The Netherlands was made up of marshlands and shallow lakes. At high tide, when the level of the North Sea rose, the coast was covered by water. Even the name of the country refers to the fact that much of the land lies below sea level. *Netherlands* means *Lowlands.*

When the ancient people weren't fishing, they spent their time trying to survive in their marshy homeland. It was impossible to farm or build a shelter on the wet land. The northwestern part of the country, where people called the Frisians lived, was so wet that it was more fit for fish than for human beings.

More than two thousand years ago the Frisians figured out a way to improve life in the marshlands. They piled up dirt and clay into mounds. These mounds, called terpen, were high enough to stick out of the water at high tide. On top of these man-made islands the Frisians constructed homes and barns. On some very large terpen, entire villages were built. Some of the terpen can still be seen today, with churches or farms standing atop them.

The Frisians also devised a way to grow a few crops in the marshlands. They used dirt and stones to wall off sections of the land. These walls, although not well made by today's standards, did help keep the sea out. The Frisians then planted crops in the walled-off areas. These dirt and stone seawalls were the country's first dikes.

Engraving of the Roman construction during their occupation of Holland

Starting in the year 58 B.C. and for about four hundred years after that—the Romans ruled The Netherlands. The Roman scientist and historian Pliny the Elder gave us this early description of the Nederlanders: "Here a miserable people live on high hills or mounds that they have made and on which they have built their huts. They are like sailors in ships when the tide is high and like shipwrecked people when the waters have again retreated."

Before the Romans were driven out of the country, the Nederlanders learned some valuable lessons from them. The Romans began the systematic and elaborate construction of dikes—along rivers as well as on the seacoast.

In the centuries after the Romans left, Nederlanders built numerous dikes to hold back the sea. The customary way was to encircle a piece of land with dikes and then drain water from it. Farms then were built on these fertile lands that once had been covered by water. Each land area taken from the sea by the building of dikes was called a polder.

A system of windmills is used to drain water from the land. This group of polder mills is in the province of South Holland.

When it rained, the low-lying polders filled with water like teacups left out in a storm. The Dutch needed a way to keep water out of the polders. In the late 1200s the first windmills were built in The Netherlands. A windmill worked like this: the wind, which is plentiful in The Netherlands, turned the big sails. The turning sails then turned a scooper in the windmill. The scooper lifted the water from the polder and hurled it across the dike.

Thousands of windmills were built, but not all were used to drain water. Some used the power of the wind to grind wheat into flour, saw wood, and make rope. Windmills were also used to send messages. When the sails of the mill were left in a certain position, it meant that the miller was taking a rest period. Other positions signified a death in the family or an upcoming marriage. The miller's wife could even send him a message that he'd better come home soon—if he knew what was good for him!

On the country's rivers, the Dutch built both dikes and dams to prevent flooding. When you see the word *dam* at the end of a Dutch city's name, you know that it was built near a river dam. For example, the city of Amsterdam grew near a dam on the Amstel River during the 1200s. Rotterdam, Edam, Zaandam, and Spaarndam are four other cities built near dammed-up rivers.

Despite the building of dikes and dams, North Sea storms still burst through from time to time. When that has happened, villages have been flooded and thousands of people have drowned. In the year 1228, an estimated 100,000 persons died in a seacoast flood. Another flood in 1287 claimed 50,000 lives. The terrible floods of the thirteenth century created a large inland arm of the sea in the northwestern part of the country. It was called the Zuider Zee. The Dutch didn't waste time worrying about this new inland sea. They built dikes around it.

Whenever The Netherlands faced the threat of a flood, "dike peace" was proclaimed. This meant that everyone was supposed to forget about arguments or differences of opinion with his or her neighbors. Every able-bodied person was expected to help reinforce the threatened dikes with sand and clay. Anyone who broke the "dike peace" helped patch up the damaged dikes in a most unpleasant way. He was killed and his body was stuffed into the broken part of the dike! This was harsh action by what are historically peace-loving people. It was also a reminder that the dikes were (and still are) as important as life itself to much of The Netherlands.

In the early 1600s a man named Jan Adriaanszoon made a science out of draining lakes. He originated a method to drain the large Beemster Lake. Until that time, only small bodies of water had been drained. Adriaanszoon's plan was to build a number of dikes and windmills. The windmills would pump the water in steps to higher and higher levels until it was transported all the way to the sea. The plan worked. The map had to be changed in 1612, when Beemster Lake became Beemster Polder. Other large lakes were pumped dry after this. For his efforts, Jan Adriaanszoon is remembered by the nickname *Leeghwater*, meaning *Empty-water*.

Technical advances also helped in the battle against the water. In 1784 a man named Steven Hoogendijk built a water pump that was powered by a steam engine. Steam-powered pumps then replaced some windmills during the 1800s. During the 1900s electricity has provided much of the power to pump water from the polders. A single electric pump can do the work of more than a hundred windmills.

In the early part of this century the Dutch decided to close off the Zuider Zee from the North Sea. Using cranes that could lift

Wieringermeer
Polder

Northeast
Polder

Markerwaard
Polder
(under
construction)

Eastern
Flevoland

Southern
Flevoland

Marken, Holland

tons of clay at a time, they built a giant dike The Zuider Zee dike
is 20 miles (32 kilometers) long and almost 100 yards (91 meters)
wide. A major highway runs along the top. With the completion
of this dike in 1932, the map had to be changed once more. The
Zuider Zee was no longer a saltwater arm of the North Sea. It was
now a freshwater lake, and it was named IJssel Lake.

Most importantly, the northwestern part of the country was
now protected from floods by the big dike. The land around IJssel
Lake was drained and turned into four big polders. They are
called Wieringermeer Polder, the Northeast Polder, Eastern
Flevoland, and Southern Flevoland. Construction began on a fifth
polder, the Markerwaard Polder. But construction was halted
temporarily because some people in The Netherlands protested its
completion. The protesters believe this polder will upset the
ecological balance in the area.

When the Dutch build a new polder, they face unique
challenges. How much should be used for agriculture? Should
new towns be built? If new towns are built what will they look
like? Who will live there? The new towns are built to have an

15

Many windmills were built to drain water. Others were built to use the power of the wind to saw wood or grind wheat.

"old" look. For example, streets are built at strange angles, just like the streets of cities that were built many years ago. Highways are given interesting curves. The government also carefully studies the people who apply to live in a new town. Certain numbers of farmers, storekeepers, doctors, teachers, and people of other professions are selected. Thus the new town will have the same variety of people that an established one has.

The result of all this dike building and polder making is that The Netherlands, over the centuries, has almost doubled its land area. Without the dikes, the dams, and the pumping stations, more than 40 percent of the country would be underwater. Because they took land from the sea, Nederlanders often repeat a statement made by the French philosopher Descartes: "God made the world, but the Dutch made Holland."

The storm surge barrier near Haringvliet is part of the Delta Plan.

After the 1953 flood the people who "made Holland" came up with a new plan to protect the southwestern part of their country. After repairing damaged dikes, they formulated the Delta Plan, a complex network of dams and dikes. This important project is scheduled for completion in 1985.

After all these centuries of dike building, the Dutch deserve some rest. But, due to geological factors, their work will never end. The Netherlands is sinking at the rate of about a foot and a half (457 millimeters) per century. To make things worse, the level of the North Sea has been rising slightly because of melting Arctic ice. Falling land and rising sea mean that the Dutch will have to continue strengthening their old dikes and building new ones if The Netherlands is to continue to exist.

Beach at Noordwijk aan Zee

Chapter 2

GEOGRAPHY, NATURAL RESOURCES, AND CLIMATE

The Netherlands (sometimes referred to as Holland) is part of the continent of Europe. It is in northwestern Europe. To the west and to the north of The Netherlands is the North Sea. Germany is to the east, Belgium to the south.

The Netherlands is a small country. Its 15,892 square miles (41,160 square kilometers) make it not much larger than Belgium. West Germany is approximately six times the size of The Netherlands. France is almost fourteen times bigger than The Netherlands.

GEOGRAPHY

The Netherlands has four land regions. They are called the Dunes, the Polders, the Sand Plains, and the Southern Uplands.

The Dunes Thousands of years ago, wind and water piled up large amounts of sand just off the western shore of The Netherlands. These sand dunes form narrow barriers which, like the dikes, help protect the country from the sea. In the northwestern part of the country the dunes form some islands, named the West Frisian Islands.

The wind can shift sand dunes about quite a bit or even blow them away altogether. Because the sand dunes help protect the coast of The Netherlands from floods, the Dutch don't want to lose them! A special kind of grass, called dune grass, has been planted to help keep the dunes in place.

The Polders Heading inland from the Dunes, you come to the second land region of The Netherlands—the Polders. This is the region that the Dutch diked off and stole from the sea. Polders are still being built in The Netherlands. Because of that, The Netherlands is growing! New polders mean that the country continually has more land and less water.

The Polders region is below sea level. When you stand in a polder field, you can look across a dike and see ships floating above the level of the field!

The Netherlands' lowest point is in the Polders region. It is called the Prins Alexander Polder, and it is 22 feet (6.7 meters) below sea level. Most spots that far below sea level are populated by fish and other sea creatures, but the one in The Netherlands is populated by people.

Because of its fertile soils, the Polders is the country's leading farming region. The biggest cities in The Netherlands also can be found in the Polders. Amsterdam, Rotterdam, and Utrecht are there. The city named The Hague lies right where the Polders region meets the Dunes.

The Sand Plains East of the Polders, the land gets hillier. The land is still low—only 100 feet (30 meters) or less above sea level in most places—but it's high compared to the Polders. The Sand Plains region gets its name from the sandy soil found there.

Although the western part of The Netherlands has always been plagued by too much water, the Sand Plains region has the

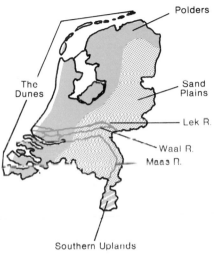

The Lek and the Waal rivers are branches of the Rhine River.

Polders

The Dunes

Sand Plains

Lek R.

Waal R.

Maas R.

Southern Uplands

This farmer uses a boat to reach his grazing cows.

opposite problem—not enough water. Irrigation ditches have been built in many places to bring water to farms. Dairy cattle, horses, and hogs are raised in the Sand Plains.

The Southern Uplands This small region in the southeastern corner of the country is the fourth and last geographical area of The Netherlands. It is the highest of the regions. The highest point in the country—Vaalser Berg—rises out of the Southern Uplands. Vaalser Berg is only 1,057 feet (322 meters) above sea level. By comparison, the highest point in nearby Switzerland is 15,203 feet (4,632 meters) above sea level. The highest point in the United States—Mount McKinley—is 20,320 feet (6,194 meters) above sea level. The Southern Uplands has fertile soils where much fruit is grown.

Shipping on the Waal River. The Ewijk Bridge is in the background.

Rivers Two major rivers flow through The Netherlands. They are the Rhine and the Maas.

The Rhine is one of Europe's most important rivers. It starts in Switzerland, forming the border between France and Germany. It flows through Germany before entering The Netherlands, on its way to the North Sea. In The Netherlands the Rhine branches into the Waal, the Lek, and the IJssel rivers.

The Maas rises in France, flows through Belgium, winds through The Netherlands, and empties into the North Sea. The Schelde River also empties into the North Sea via The Netherlands.

The rivers are important means of transportation. Canals connect the country's rivers to each other and to the North Sea. Products from other European countries are transported by boat to The Netherlands along these rivers and canals. Some of the products are used within The Netherlands. Others are shipped from Netherlands' seaports to other countries. Rotterdam is the biggest seaport in the world. Netherlands' products also go by boat through the rivers and canals to France, Germany, Switzerland, and beyond.

Canals in Marken (above) and in the village of Giethoorn in Overijssel province (left) are important means of transportation.

Petrochemical storage area in Rotterdam Harbor

NATURAL RESOURCES

The Netherlands has a wide variety of natural resources—under the ground, on the land, and in the sea.

Of the country's mining products, natural gas is the most valuable. Natural gas is needed to heat the world's homes and to cook food. The Netherlands is one of the world's top five countries in natural gas production. Natural gas is exported as far south as Italy.

Oil (petroleum) is also found in the country. It is needed to run cars and machinery. However, The Netherlands does not produce enough for its own consumption. It must import oil from other countries.

Salt is another of the country's mining products. In the Sand Plains, hot water is pumped into the underground salt reserves. The salt gets mixed in with the water. The liquid is then pumped back up, the water is evaporated, and only the salt is left. Clay—used to make bricks and pottery—is also mined in The Netherlands.

Harvesting crops in southern Holland

The fertile soil in the Polders is one of the country's most valuable natural treasures. Farmers raise a variety of crops and flowers in the rich soil.

Compared to other nations, The Netherlands has few forests. Less than 10 percent of The Netherlands is wooded, with most of the forests in the center of the country. The trees are considered a precious resource. The government owns most of them. For each tree that dies or gets burned, a new one is planted. People who want to cut down trees to build a house on their own land must get special approval from the government. They then are required to plant new trees on their property.

Eels are a favorite food.

Swimming in the country's water are another important resource: fish. For centuries Dutch fishermen have caught herring in the North Sea. The herring business was so important to Amsterdam's growth that once people used to say "Amsterdam was built on herring bones." Before the saltwater Zuider Zee was converted into IJssel Lake, herring were caught there, too. But when IJssel Lake became a freshwater lake, the herring disappeared. Many of the fishermen moved away from IJssel Lake. However, the ones who stayed found that freshwater eels came to live in the lake. Today, fishermen catch eels there and in other lakes and rivers of The Netherlands.

CLIMATE

The Netherlands has a mild climate. Its summers aren't very hot and its winters aren't very cold. The temperatures are usually in the 60s (about 16° Celsius) during the summer and in the 30s (about -1° Celsius) during the winter. There are no mountains to stop the winds in The Netherlands. This results in similar weather throughout the country at any given time.

The sea and the wind combine to keep the climate mild. In the winter, the sea is warmer than the land. The west wind blows that warmer sea air over The Netherlands, providing a free heating system for the country. In the summer, the sea is cooler than the land. That same west wind blows the cool air off the sea, providing free air conditioning.

The wind usually comes from the west, but not always. An east wind in winter means very cold weather and snow. An east summer wind brings warm, dry weather.

In a number of landscape paintings by Dutch artists, the sky is usually portrayed as cloudy. That is because The Netherlands is a very cloudy country. The predominant west wind picks up moisture from the sea. That moisture turns into clouds.

When the clouds are extremely low, the country has fog. The lowlands, particularly in the autumn, are often blanketed by fog. Higher clouds bear rain. The average 30 inches (762 millimeters) of rain per year make The Netherlands a rainy country. The rainstorms have their good and bad sides. When not too heavy, they help the crops and flowers grow. But the gale force winds and huge rainstorms sweeping inland from the North Sea bring with them the danger of flood.

The different customs, language, dialects, and traditional costumes reflect the different regions of the Netherlands. The couple (left) come from Volendam. The four children (below) dress as they once did in Marken.

Chapter 3

THE HISTORY OF
THE NETHERLANDS

PREHISTORIC PEOPLE

It is thought that people first came to The Netherlands from central Europe. Evidence of human beings dating back eighteen thousand years has been found on Texel Island. The earliest Nederlanders made weapons and tools out of stone. They moved about as they hunted and fished for food. By six thousand years ago people had settled permanently in The Netherlands.

In the northern part of the country are monuments built by the Nederlanders of four thousand years ago. They are piles of very large rocks, erected as memorials to the dead. They are known as the Giants' Graves, or Hunenbedden.

By about twenty-five hundred years ago a number of tribes had settled in The Netherlands. The Frisians, builders of the terpen (mounds), lived in the northwestern region still called Friesland. Other tribes settled elsewhere. Tribes that came from central and western Europe were known as the Celtic tribes. Those that came from northern Europe were called the Germanic tribes.

The people of these various tribes differed in their languages and customs. They looked different from one another. To this day the people in different regions of The Netherlands maintain varying customs, language dialects, and manners of dress.

Julius Caesar

THE ROMAN ERA

A Greek named Pytheas was one of the first explorers in The Netherlands. Pytheas arrived in about 325 B.C., observed the tides that covered the coast, and later described the place as "the end of the earth." The Greeks thought that Pytheas had made up a tall tale. For more than 250 years outsiders showed no interest in The Netherlands.

During the century before the birth of Christ, the Romans were busy conquering much of the known world. In the year 58 B.C. Romans under the leadership of Julius Caesar finally made it to "the end of the earth." They entered The Netherlands, as well as the lands that are now Belgium and Luxembourg. This entire region was known as the Low Countries. The people of the Low Countries fought back, but they were beaten by the huge and well-organized Roman army. The Romans established themselves as rulers.

Drawing of Clovis done from a reclining statue made for his tomb. Clovis was king of the Franks from 481 to 511. Clovis defeated the last great Roman army in Gaul in 486. He was the first Germanic king to become a Christian.

The Romans taught Nederlanders how to build better dikes. They also constructed highways and towns. However, the Nederlanders revolted against the Romans from time to time. One early revolt was by the Frisians in the year A.D. 28 when they murdered some tax collectors.

THE RULE OF THE FRANKS

The Nederlanders weren't strong enough to drive the Romans out. But by the 400s the Roman Empire was falling apart. The Romans were pushed out of The Netherlands by a Germanic people called the Franks. The Franks eventually extended their kingdom to include what are now The Netherlands, Belgium, France, and part of Germany.

The Franks brought Christianity to The Netherlands. The first Frankish king to become a Christian was named Clovis. A later

Frankish king, the famous Charlemagne (742-814), converted most of the Nederlanders to Christianity. Charlemagne built his capital in the city of Aachen, near where the borders of The Netherlands, West Germany, and Belgium meet today.

After Charlemagne died, the Frankish kingdom weakened. It was divided into the East Frankish Kingdom (now Germany) and the West Frankish Kingdom (now France). Starting in 870, The Netherlands was under the rule of the East Frankish Kingdom. Not only were Nederlanders ruled by outsiders, but also they were invaded by warriors from Scandinavian countries to the north.

For protection, some of the people went to work for noblemen. The noblemen built castles on large pieces of land. People built small houses on the noblemen's land, worked for them, and paid them rent and taxes. Towns, each like a little kingdom, grew up around the noblemen's castles.

During and after the 1100s, new polders were created. The Netherlands steadily increased in size as the coastal lakes and swamps were diked in. On the new land, people built houses, farms, and towns. Amsterdam, Rotterdam, and The Hague—now the three biggest cities in The Netherlands—all were founded during the 1200s.

In the growing towns a new group of people evolved. They were people who worked for themselves. Some made ships. Others operated fishing fleets. Still others manufactured cloth and a variety of other products. The manufactured goods were loaded on ships and then sold in foreign lands. The shipowners, merchants, and businessmen became wealthy. Many had independent spirits and hated being ruled by a foreign power. They spoke of freeing their land. It took several centuries— including many years of war—to accomplish this.

Charlemagne (left) was crowned king of the Franks in 771. Philip II of Spain (right)

THE WAR FOR INDEPENDENCE

During the 1300s and 1400s, the dukes of Burgundy from
France took control of The Netherlands. One of those dukes,
Charles, became king of Spain in 1516. As Charles V he ruled over
more European countries than any other monarch before or since.
The Netherlands was one of the countries in his kingdom.

Charles V was a Catholic. So was his son, Philip II, who ruled
after him. In The Netherlands—and throughout Europe—many
persons had become Protestants during the 1500s. King Philip
ordered many Protestants put to death. He took away the rights of
those he spared.

This was the last straw for many Nederlanders. They had been ruled by the Romans, then the Franks, the Germans, the French, and now the Spanish. The religious persecution by the Spanish finally caused a long but eventually successful war for independence.

The revolution began in 1568. The Nederlanders were led by one of their noblemen named William, the prince of Orange. William was also called "William the Silent" because he thought quite a bit before speaking. The Spanish attacked Dutch cities and killed Nederlanders. But, led by William the Silent, the Dutch won victories at sea.

In 1573, the Spanish surrounded the city of Leiden. Although the Spanish siege lasted for months, the people of Leiden wouldn't give up, even after seven thousand of them had died of hunger and disease. In an attempt to flood the Spanish from their positions around Leiden, William the Silent ordered the dikes cut. This action—plus a fortunate storm—drove the Spanish out of Leiden. On the morning of October 3, 1574, a young boy looked out over the city wall and saw that the Spanish were gone. October 3 is still celebrated as the day of independence in Leiden. To reward the people for their heroism, William the Silent offered either freedom from taxation or the construction of a university. The people chose a university as their reward. So the University of Leiden was founded in 1575.

An unusual episode occurred when the Spanish fleet was sailing near the town of Enkhuizen during the winter of 1573. The weather turned very cold and the Zuider Zee froze. The Spanish ships were caught in the ice. The Nederlanders waited until the ice was thick enough, and then sent out horsemen to capture the Spanish ships. This was probably the only sea battle in history won on horseback.

William the Silent was the prince of Orange. He is called the "Father of the Netherlands."

Not all Nederlanders joined in the fight against Spain. Some Catholics in the south remained loyal to Spain. But in 1579, by the Union of Utrecht, The Netherlands' seven northern provinces agreed to cooperate in their efforts to drive the Spanish soldiers from their land. The Union of Utrecht was their "Declaration of Independence." Two years later they declared The Netherlands a free and independent country. William the Silent was named head of both the government and the army. Today William the Silent is remembered as the "Father of The Netherlands" because of his importance in the formation of the country.

The war, begun in 1568, lasted for eighty years, and so it is known as the Eighty Years' War. Weakened by a series of wars with other nations, Spain finally recognized The Netherlands' independence in 1648.

35

Sketch showing one of the Arctic explorations of Willem Barents

THE GOLDEN AGE

The seventeenth century is remembered as The Netherlands' "Golden Age." During that century The Netherlands was the leading country in many fields.

Its merchants and huge fleets of ships made it the world's leading nation in shipping. By 1625 The Netherlands was engaged in more shipping than every other country of the world combined. Its ships went to ports around the world and brought back spices, tea, and silk. Dutch merchants and traders became very wealthy. Amsterdam became the leading trading center in Europe and also an important city for banking.

During the 1600s—and also a few years before—Dutch explorers ventured to the far corners of the world. There are many places on the globe named for them.

From 1594 to 1596 Willem Barents explored a sea in the far north. It later was named the Barents Sea. In 1596 Barents and his crew explored the Svalbard Islands, not far from the North Pole. When their ship got stuck in the ice, Barents and his men became the first Europeans to spend the winter so close to the North Pole.

Henry Hudson (left)
Abel Tasman (right)

In 1609 Henry Hudson, an Englishman working for the Dutch, became the first European to explore the Hudson River in what is now New York State. The next year he discovered Hudson Bay in Canada. In 1615 the Dutch sailor Willem Schouten discovered Cape Horn, at the southern tip of South America. He named it for Hoorn, his hometown in The Netherlands. In 1642 Abel Tasman discovered New Zealand and Tasmania. New Zealand was named for a province in The Netherlands. Tasmania and the nearby Tasman Sea were named, of course, for Abel Tasman.

Many areas visited by Dutch explorers were claimed by The Netherlands. In America, the Dutch claimed parts of what are now the states of New York, New Jersey, Delaware, and Connecticut. They sent settlers and traders to the region, which they called New Netherland. In 1624 the Dutch built Fort Orange (now Albany, New York), their first permanent settlement in New Netherland. In 1626 the Dutch bought Manhattan Island from the Indians for about $24. They built a town called New Amsterdam, which grew into New York City.

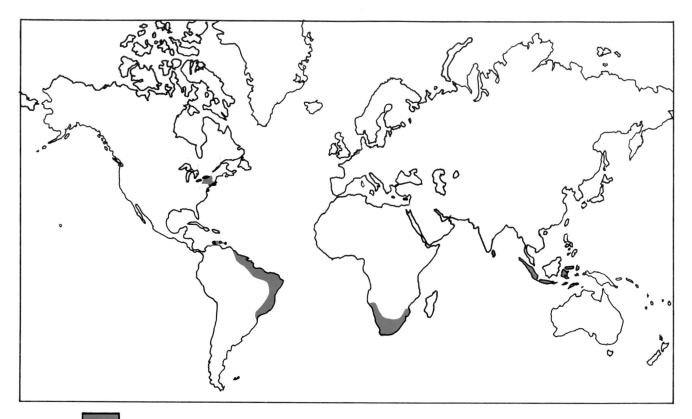

Colonial territories in the early 1600s held by The Dutch

Many city and place names in the United States show the influence of Dutch settlement. Brooklyn, Harlem, Yonkers, and Rensselaer in New York State; Batavia, Friesland, and New Amsterdam in Wisconsin; Holland in Michigan; and the Broadkill and Murderkill rivers in Delaware all have Dutch names.

During the Golden Age, Nederlanders settled many other regions of the world. In the 1620s The Netherlands took control of Indonesia and its rich trade in spices. In 1630 the Dutch claimed part of the South American country of Brazil. In 1634 they captured a group of islands in the Caribbean Sea. The red, white, and blue Dutch flag was soon flying over these islands, which were named the Netherlands Antilles. By the 1650s Dutch Boers (farmers) were settling in South Africa. In 1667 the Dutch traded what is now New York State to the English. In return they received the South American country of Surinam.

When a country controls foreign lands, it is called a colonial power. The Netherlands was one of the great colonial powers of the seventeenth century. There were few regions of the world that didn't feel the influence of Dutch traders and settlers.

While the Dutch were colonizing and trading abroad, The Netherlands was producing an incredible number of gifted people back home. Many of the world's best artists lived in The Netherlands during the seventeenth century. Rembrandt, born in Leiden, was the greatest of them. Frans Hals, Jan Vermeer, and Jacob van Ruisdael were three other famous Dutch artists of the seventeenth century. The prosperity of the merchants and traders helped the arts to flourish. Rich businessmen wanted portraits of themselves and their families. They paid artists large sums to paint such works.

William the Silent had founded The Netherlands' first university at Leiden in 1575. Universities also were founded at Utrecht, Groningen, and Harderwijk. (The University at Harderwijk closed in 1812.) They became known throughout the world for producing scientists, philosophers, and other great thinkers. Christiaan Huygens, the scientist who discovered the rings of Saturn, studied at the University of Leiden. Law expert Hugo Grotius was graduated from the University of Leiden at the age of fifteen. Philosopher Baruch Spinoza and scientist Anton van Leeuwenhoek were just two other famous Nederlanders of the Golden Age.

During its Golden Age The Netherlands also displayed a religious tolerance that was rare at the time. The Netherlands was the only nation in Europe where Jewish people were treated as equal citizens. Protestants from Belgium and France also went to The Netherlands because of the country's religious freedom. After the Pilgrims fled England—and before they sailed to America— they lived in The Netherlands for a dozen years for the sake of religious freedom.

A leader in art, science, philosophy, education, and trade—this was The Netherlands during its Golden Age.

WARS AND MORE WARS

During the 1600s and 1700s, and on into the 1800s, European nations fought an incredible number of wars. These wars were waged over various lands and also to determine who would rule the seas. Because The Netherlands was rich, strong, and a great sea power, it was a prime target for attack.

Between 1652 and 1674 The Netherlands fought three sea wars against England. England wanted to replace The Netherlands as the world's leading shipping country. The English couldn't defeat the Dutch fleets at sea, however.

During the last of these three wars, France joined with England in an attack against The Netherlands. The Dutch won sea battles, but French soldiers captured some Dutch cities. When the French marched toward Amsterdam in 1672, the Dutch cut dikes to flood the land. This tactic almost backfired. During the winter the water surrounding Amsterdam froze, and the French resumed their march. Fortunately the weather turned warmer, the ice melted, and the French had to retreat through the mud.

Just a few years later England joined The Netherlands in two wars against France. They were fought from 1688 to 1697 and from 1702 to 1713. Although The Netherlands was again victorious, it was financially drained by these wars. This allowed England, during the 1700s, to become a greater sea power than The Netherlands. During that century Dutch trade lessened, and the country lost a number of its overseas colonies.

The Netherlands supported the American colonies during their war of independence. This led to what is called the Fourth English War (1780-1784), when England severely beat the Dutch fleet. Then in 1795 French soldiers marched swiftly into The Netherlands. Not only had The Netherlands lost many of its overseas colonies, but also the country itself now was under pro-French rule. French troops were used by the Dutch "Patriot Party" to set up a new government. They called it the Batavian Republic and ruled until the Dutch drove the French out in 1813.

After Napoleon and the French were defeated, The Netherlands and Belgium were united as one country, called the Kingdom of The Netherlands. The Kingdom of The Netherlands was no longer a republic. It was ruled by a king. This union lasted from 1815 to 1830. But then in 1830 Belgium revolted and declared its independence. It became a separate country from The Netherlands, as it remains today.

THE REVIVAL OF THE NETHERLANDS

Beginning in about 1870, The Netherlands entered a new period of growth. It was nothing like the Golden Age, but it was an improvement over the years of warfare.

Canals were dug linking Amsterdam and Rotterdam with the

41

Locks on the Amstel River near the Magere Brug, a drawbridge, in Amsterdam. Magerebrug means "thin or skinny bridge." This one is wide enough for only a single automobile.

North Sea. In these and other cities, factories were built for the manufacture of many products. In the early 1900s the steel industry grew in importance. The making of chemicals, cloth, and ships became major industries, too. Many goods manufactured in The Netherlands were shipped to other countries.

Meanwhile, farmers learned improved methods of growing crops. Chemical fertilizers were used in the eastern and southern parts of the country. For the first time farmers could grow a variety of crops in the sandy soil. Although in the present century industry has overtaken farming as the Nederlanders' main way of making a living, farmers still produce vast quantities of milk and many crops.

In this century one more war ravaged The Netherlands, as well as much of the rest of the world. This was World War II (1939-1945). In May of 1940 German troops attacked The Netherlands. This time water could not be used to stop the enemy, because the Germans attacked from the air. Most of central Rotterdam was destroyed by bombs dropped from planes. For the next five years German troops occupied The Netherlands. The Nazi Germans, who had a particular hatred for Jewish people, put more than 100,000 Jewish Nederlanders to death.

Although The Netherlands was captured, the Dutch navy helped the United States and the other Allies win the war. "Underground" groups within The Netherlands also fought the Germans in every way they could. By 1945 Germany and the other Axis countries were beaten. Although The Netherlands was now free of Germany and was also on the winning side, the country had suffered terribly. Almost 300,000 Nederlanders had died in the war. Cities, factories, and shipyards were in ruin and had to be rebuilt.

Long ago, The Netherlands freed itself from Spain. In the past half century, the country's colonies have sought that same freedom. In late 1949, after several years of fighting, Indonesia freed itself from The Netherlands. In 1954 Surinam in South America and the Netherlands Antilles islands in the Caribbean Sea became self-governing territories. In 1975 Surinam became a completely independent nation.

Today The Netherlands has no colonies remaining. However, one of its former territories is now a sister country. This country, the Netherlands Antilles, is made up of islands in the Caribbean Sea. The Netherlands and the Netherlands Antilles together form what is called the Kingdom of The Netherlands. Each country has its own government.

Her Majesty Queen Beatrix, His Royal Highness Prince Claus and their children: Prince Willem-Alexander, Prince Johan Friso, and Prince Constantijn

Chapter 4

GOVERNMENT

The Dutch flag is composed of three stripes colored red, white, and blue The flag was first used in about the year 1630. The country's national anthem is "Wilhelmus van Nassouwe" (William of Nassau). It is thought to have been written in 1568 when The Netherlands began its fight for freedom from Spain. The form of government in The Netherlands is called a constitutional monarchy.

Constitutional means that the government is based on a set of laws. Parts of the Dutch constitution were first written back in 1579. *Monarchy* means that the head of government is a monarch—a queen or king. Since 1980 the monarch in The Netherlands has been Queen Beatrix Wilhelmina Armgard. Queen Beatrix is a descendant of William the Silent, who helped free The Netherlands back in the 1500s.

Queens and kings in The Netherlands are not crowned. A crown symbolizes great power. Nederlanders believe that the people should be the real rulers of the country. In fact, although the queen signs laws, appoints judges and some other officials, and is respected and honored by the people, she has little power. Most of the lawmakers in The Netherlands are elected directly by the people. So, despite being called a constitutional monarchy, The Netherlands is basically a democracy. This means that, by voting in elections, the people decide the course their country will follow.

NATIONAL GOVERNMENT

The national government works on laws and problems that affect the whole country. Although the official capital is still Amsterdam, the national government headquarters is at The Hague, a city in the southwestern part of the country.

The prime minister, who is appointed by the monarch, is the head of the national government. The prime minister chooses the heads of the various national departments. These departments include the Ministry of Justice, the Ministry of Defense, the Ministry of Foreign Affairs, The Ministry of Transport and Public Works, and the Ministry of Education and Science.

As in the United States, The Netherlands has two houses of lawmakers in its national government. In the United States the two are called the Senate and the House of Representatives. In The Netherlands they are called the First Chamber and the Second Chamber of the States General, or congress.

The First Chamber has 75 members and the Second Chamber has 150. Both chambers can pass laws that have already been proposed. But the Second Chamber is considered the more important of the two because only its members can propose laws.

The national government of The Netherlands is one that cares about people. For example, the government assists senior citizens with medical care, income, and housing. A national sick fund provides income for people who are ill and an insurance fund provides assistance for those who have lost their jobs.

Statistics show that the national government has done a fine job of meeting the people's needs. The number of infant deaths in The Netherlands is among the lowest in the world. The average life expectancy in the country (nearly seventy-nine years for women,

Government buildings in The Hague

Open-air market in The Hague

seventy-two years for men) is the second highest in the world—just behind Norway. During their long lives, Nederlanders enjoy one of the highest standards of living of any people on earth.

PROVINCIAL GOVERNMENT

The Netherlands is composed of eleven provinces. Each of the provinces has its own government. The monarch appoints a commissioner for each province. The commissioner acts as a chief executive and provides a direct link with the monarch.

In addition, the people of each province elect what is called a provincial state. This body of representatives passes laws which affect the people of the entire province. It also elects the representatives for the First Chamber.

LOCAL GOVERNMENT

Every city and town in The Netherlands also has its own government. The chief official in each city or town is called the burgomaster. The burgomaster is appointed by the monarch. The city council, elected by the voters in the city, passes laws and keeps an eye on things such as public transportation, street repairs, and other matters that relate to the welfare of the city.

The Netherlands also has special political officials to care for the dikes and polders. Each polder—or set of neighboring polders—is called a waterschap (watership). There are hundreds of waterschappen in The Netherlands. A waterschap council is in charge of the polders, dikes, canals, and pumps in a particular area. The waterschappen councils are the oldest governmental institutions in The Netherlands.

Aerial view of Amsterdam

Chapter 5

CITIES OF THE
NETHERLANDS

Long ago, all Nederlanders lived on farms or in small fishing settlements. The first major towns were built during the 1200s by merchants and traders. By the 1600s there were dozens of cities and towns in The Netherlands; Amsterdam was the third largest city in all of Europe.

As manufacturing grew in importance during the last hundred years, many people moved to the cities to work in the factories. Today, 85 percent of all Nederlanders live in cities. Only 15 percent live on farms or in small villages.

AMSTERDAM: THE CAPITAL CITY

During the 1200s a town grew up around a wooden dam built on the Amstel River. Called Amstel Dam at first, the town's name later was changed to Amsterdam. During the Golden Age,

Row of houses in central Amsterdam

Amsterdam was the world's leading trading center as well as a great banking and cultural center. The capital of the Netherlands, Amsterdam still is important in all these fields. It is also nearly tied with Rotterdam as the country's most populous city.

Amsterdam lies a few feet below sea level. When planes arrive at Amsterdam's nearby airport—called Schiphol—they are actually landing on what used to be the bottom of a lake.

Because of the moist ground in Amsterdam, many of the city's buildings were constructed atop wooden posts. In places where buildings weren't erected, canals were dug to accommodate boats. The city has about 550 bridges (more than any other city in the world) so that people can cross the canals. The bridges, tree-lined canals, and old red-brick buildings make Amsterdam one of the world's prettiest cities.

One interesting aspect of Amsterdam is the way its builders used every bit of available space. The old houses stand close

The outer dock and St. Nicholas Church in Amsterdam (left) and Rembrandt's house (right)

together. The staircases in many of them are so narrow that large items can't be carried upstairs. That is why there are hoists atop many of the houses. Large objects are raised up the sides of the houses by pulleys and then moved in through the windows. Many of these old houses were built slanting forward towards the street, so that large objects wouldn't bang against the walls while being lifted.

There are many interesting old buildings in Amsterdam. The Old Church of St. Nicholas was built in about the year 1300. The New Church, built in 1408, is where the country's queens and kings are inaugurated. Joost van den Vondel, the country's most famous writer, is buried in the New Church.

The house of the great artist Rembrandt can be seen in Amsterdam. Just a block away is the house where the famous philosopher Spinoza was born.

Amsterdam is laced by canals. Boats often take tourists on a water journey through the city.

Amsterdam has many fine museums. The Rijksmuseum, with its works by Rembrandt, Vermeer, and Hals, is one of the best art museums in the world. The city's Concertgebouw Orchestra is one of the world's great symphony orchestras.

The people of Amsterdam make their living in a variety of ways. Many work in banking and insurance. Airplanes, electronics equipment, chemicals, foods, and steel are some of the products made there.

Because Amsterdam had a growing population with limited space for them to live, officials during the 1930s devised a plan to make sure there would be room for everybody. This plan, which covers the city's development to the year 2000, involves building suburbs on the outskirts of town. One such suburb, called Bijlmermeer, was designed to house 100,000 people.

Peace Monument in Dam Square commemorates those who died in World War II.
The Royal Palace (former City Hall) is in the center of the background.

Molenwijk Housing Development (above) was constructed after World War II.
The majority of Nederlanders prefer to live in single family homes with front
and back gardens. Below: A view of the Herengracht by night

Amsterdam

Amsterdam is the most populous city
in The Netherlands. It has
pleasant parks, such as Vondel
Park (top), and busy commercial
streets, such as Reguliers
Dwarsstraat (left). The city grew
west from the harbor at Amsterdam.

Gardens at the Peace Palace

The Hague

THE HAGUE: CENTER FOR GOVERNMENT

In 1248 a nobleman built a castle in a forest used for hunting. The town that grew up around the castle was named The Hague (The Hedge). During the 1500s The Hague became the seat of government in The Netherlands when representatives of cities and provinces gathered there to be near the prince of Orange. Amsterdam, because of its importance, is the official "capital." But The Hague is now where the country's lawmakers meet.

Many government buildings, including the houses of parliament, are located in The Hague. Queen Beatrix chose an ancient palace in the city for her official residence.

The Hague is a very historic city. The Knights' Hall, where the queen opens each year's government sessions with a speech, was built in about 1280. The city has ancient churches and large museums. The canals and wide tree-lined streets make The Hague quite a lovely city as well.

The Hague is known as the "Peace City." Important peace conferences have been held there for centuries. The International Court of Justice has its headquarters in the Peace Palace built by Andrew Carnegie, an American millionaire. This is a United Nations court that settles legal disputes between countries.

The Palace of Peace, also frequently called Peace Palace, at The Hague

Lijnbaan shopping mall in Rotterdam

Amsterdam
Utrecht
Rotterdam

ROTTERDAM: A REBUILT CITY

Back in the late 1200s, a fishing village, called Rotterdam, was founded on a new polder just 13 miles (21 kilometers) from The Hague.

When a waterway was completed connecting Rotterdam to the North Sea in 1872, the city became an important seaport. Because of its importance, Rotterdam was attacked by German bombers during World War II. In several hours, more than 1,000 people were killed and more than 35,000 buildings were blown to pieces. A famous statue, *Destroyed City*, reminds people of what happened to Rotterdam during World War II.

After the war, Rotterdam was rebuilt with big new office buildings and wide streets. Because of this recent construction, Rotterdam is one of The Netherlands' most modern cities.

Harbor at Rotterdam. This is the older, "inner" harbor. Larger harbor facilities lie downstream.

Rotterdam's port was also rebuilt and enlarged. Rotterdam is now the busiest seaport in all the world. Giant ships, bearing goods for all of Europe, go in and out of the city's harbor. Goods made in Europe are sent out from Rotterdam's harbor to other cities of the world.

Rotterdam is an important shipbuilding city. Chemicals, cigars, sugar, paints, and liquor are some of the city's other products.

The St. Laurens Church is one of the most famous landmarks in Rotterdam. Built in the fifteenth century, it is one of the few old buildings that survived the bombing of World War II. Another of the city's landmarks is a seventeenth-century statue of the philosopher Erasmus, who was born in Rotterdam.

Canal in Utrecht, the tower of the Dom Cathedral is in the background.

UTRECHT: CITY OF SPIRES AND BRIDGES

Almost two thousand years ago the Romans built a fortress in the Utrecht region. In the seventh century, one of the first Christian churches in the northern Netherlands was built in Utrecht. It was called St. Martin's Cathedral. St. Martin's was destroyed by fire in 1253, but Utrecht has many other ancient churches still standing. Janskerk was built in 1040 and Pieterskerk went up in 1048. Another famous church, the Dom, was destroyed by a hurricane in 1674. Only its tower survived. Because of all these churches—and because so many bridges cross its canals—Utrecht is nicknamed the "City of Spires and Bridges."

Castle of De Haar, near Utrecht

Adrian VI, a pope of the Catholic church, was born in Utrecht in 1459. His house is now used as a government building. Until John Paul II of Poland became pope in 1978, Adrian VI was the last non-Italian pope.

Utrecht has special historical significance for Nederlanders. In 1579, when Spain still ruled The Netherlands, representatives from seven provinces met in Utrecht. They declared that they would work together to drive the Spanish from their country. Their agreement, called the Union of Utrecht, was an important step in the birth of The Netherlands as an independent nation. Some historians feel that the Union of Utrecht served as a model for the United States' Declaration of Independence.

LEIDEN: CENTER FOR LEARNING

To reward the people of Leiden for their heroic stand against Spain, William the Silent offered them a choice. They could either be free of taxes or have a university. They chose the university. Since the founding of its university in 1575, Leiden, located just 16 miles (26 kilometers) northeast of The Hague, has been an important center for learning.

Astronomer Christiaan Huygens, medical doctor Hermann Boerhaave, and international law expert Hugo Grotius were just three famous persons who attended the University of Leiden. The artist Rembrandt was born in Leiden.

Leiden also has an important connection to American history. The Pilgrims lived there before sailing to America on the *Mayflower*. They went there for the same religious freedom that so many others have found in The Netherlands.

The following are other important cities of The Netherlands:

Arnhem: A city on the Rhine River that was devastated by German bombs during World War II. Not far from Arnhem is the Kröller-Müller National Museum, where many van Gogh and Mondrian paintings are exhibited.

Breda: A city in the southern part of the country. A treaty signed in Breda in 1667 turned New Netherland (now part of the United States) over to the English.

Dordrecht: This very old town was badly damaged in the St. Elizabeth Flood of 1421. Today it is a major shipbuilding city.

Eindhoven: This was a small village when Anton Philips built his electric bulb factory in 1891. The Philips Lamp Company is now one of the largest companies in the world. Eindhoven is now one of The Netherlands' largest cities.

Enschede: A big textile (clothmaking) city in the far eastern part of the country.

Groningen: Home of the University of Groningen, one of the largest universities in the country. The city has many lovely old buildings, including the fifteenth-century St. Martin's Church.

Haarlem: This city is in the middle of The Netherlands' main tulip-growing region. Haarlem was home to the artist, Frans Hals, whose works are displayed in the Frans Hals Museum.

Hilversum: The country's radio and TV headquarters and broadcasting facilities are located in this city.

Maastricht: Lying on the Maas River near the southeastern corner of the country, this city has churches dating back five hundred years and more. Near Maastricht are some mine tunnels where twenty thousand people and great art works were hidden during World War II.

Nijmegen: Charlemagne, king of the Franks, once lived in this city on the Waal River.

Tilburg: Located in the southern part of the country, this city produces textiles and leather.

Zaandam: Long ago, Zaandam was part of a big windmill region. Although many have been dismantled, windmills still can be seen in the Zaandam area.

Above: Airborn Cemetery at Oosterbeek near Arnhem
Below: Nijmegen on the river Waal

Above: Horse-drawn cart taking horses to the races near Eindhoven
Below: Cheese and nut shop at Maastricht and the organ
in the Church of Saint Bavo in Haarlem

Container terminal at Amsterdam Harbor

Chapter 6

HOW THE PEOPLE MAKE THEIR LIVING

For hundreds of years, The Netherlands was mainly an agricultural country. But in the present century that has changed. Today, more people make their living in manufacturing than in any other way. One in three persons in The Netherlands is involved in manufacturing.

MANUFACTURING PRODUCTS

The making of metal is one of the country's main businesses. About forty thousand Nederlanders work in this industry.

The Netherlands has a major problem when it comes to making finished metal. It doesn't have raw ore. For example, it lacks the iron ore needed to make finished iron and steel. The country has solved this problem by importing the raw ores. They are turned into finished metals in The Netherlands' mills.

Traditional dress of the guild is worn at the weekly cheese market in Alkmaar, north of Amsterdam.

Iron and steel are the main metals that the country produces. There are big mills for making these metals in the North Sea town of IJmuiden, not far from Amsterdam. Other metals processed in The Netherlands include aluminum, tin, copper, lead, and zinc.

The processing and packaging of food is another major industry in The Netherlands. The country is world famous for its dairy products, particularly cheese. Just as raw iron is needed to make steel, milk is needed to make cheese. The Netherlands has no problem in this regard. The milk comes from the country's millions of cows. Raw milk is made into packaged milk, butter, and cheese in dairies.

Several famous cheeses are named after Netherlands towns where they were first produced. Edam cheese originated in the town of Edam. Gouda cheese was first produced in Gouda. Eggs, sugar, chocolate, tea, coffee, beer, and meat are some of the other foods processed and packaged in Netherlands' factories.

Three types of commercial aircraft built by Fokker

The making of vehicles is another thriving industry. The Netherlands has long been an important shipbuilder. The vessels range in size from huge supertankers to yachts, tugboats, and sailboats. The Fokker Company, a Dutch aircraft manufacturer, makes airplanes for many European and American airlines. Royal Dutch Airlines(KLM) — the oldest airline on earth — gets some of its planes from Fokker. Cars, trucks, buses, and bicycles are other vehicles made in The Netherlands.

The electronics industry has seen tremendous growth in recent years. Electronics products made in The Netherlands include computers and X-ray equipment. Much of the country's electronics equipment is made by Philips, one of the largest companies of any kind in the world. The chemical industry has also become important. Chemical products include plastics, soaps, paints, and fertilizers. Other Netherlands products include clothing, cloth, books and other printed materials, paper, cardboard, shoes, and leather goods.

Some of these products are bought and used by people in The Netherlands. Others are packed aboard ships, barges, trucks, trains, and airplanes and then exported to other countries.

AGRICULTURAL PRODUCTS

Only about 6 percent of all the people in The Netherlands make their living by farming. Yet despite the dwindling number of farmers, farm output has steadily increased. This is partly because of modern machinery.

The raising of dairy cattle is the country's most important farm activity. The plentiful rainfall, mild climate, and the grassy pastures are perfect for dairy cows. There are four million dairy cows in The Netherlands—about one for every four persons. In the old days, the cows were milked by hand. Today machines milk most of the dairy herds. The dairy cows produce about 20 billion pounds (9 billion kilograms) of milk per year—enough to make a good-sized lake of milk. However, the milk is used for better purposes—to make butter, cheese, and packaged milk.

A famous breed of dairy cow was first raised in The Netherlands' province of Friesland. It is the Holstein-Friesian breed. It's the most popular kind of dairy cow in The Netherlands and also in the United States.

Beef cattle, pigs, chickens that lay eggs, chickens that wind up in broilers, and sheep are other livestock raised on Dutch farms. Texel sheep, which originated on The Netherlands' Texel Island, are still raised there.

The country's farmers grow many crops. Wheat, barley, rye, oats, potatoes, and sugar beets are among the main ones. Lettuce, cucumbers, tomatoes, mushrooms, apples, pears, cherries, strawberries, and grapes also are grown by Netherlands farmers. Some vegetables are grown inside greenhouses so that they can get proper heat, water, and sunlight all year long.

Flower fields in bloom near Haarlem

The Netherlands is famous for another "crop"—flowers. In the spring the region between Haarlem and Leiden looks like a giant, colorful patchwork quilt. The flowers are raised mainly for their bulbs. Several *thousand* kinds of tulips are grown in the country. Hyacinths, daffodils, and crocuses also are grown for their bulbs. Bulbs from The Netherlands are planted in gardens large and small all over the world. Many of the fresh cut flowers sold in markets around the world are flown in fresh from The Netherlands each day.

Volendam Harbor

FISHING

Although today only a few thousand Nederlanders fish for a living, their catch is large and varied. Herring is one of the main catches. Mussels, mackerel, cod, haddock, shrimp, and oysters are other seafoods brought back by fishermen.

In Breskens, Urk, IJmuiden, and other fishing ports, food companies buy the fish at special auctions. The companies then package the fish.

The Netherlands is a perfect example of how people of various occupations depend on one another. Cheesemakers need the farmers who raise cows. Fish packers depend on fishermen. Fishermen need shipbuilders, and dairy farmers rely on factory workers who produce farm machinery.

GOVERNMENT JOBS AND OTHER OCCUPATIONS

Nederlanders have always been good at cooperation and planning. In other words, they're good at governing themselves. They've *had* to be good. It takes amazing degrees of cooperation and planning just to keep the water out of their country.

Today The Netherlands has committees and government offices to cover just about every aspect of national and private life. In addition to the national, provincial, and local lawmakers, many other persons are hired by the government to do research on such topics as energy, pollution problems, and water control.

The Delta Project, begun in the 1950s and scheduled for completion in 1985, is a good example of how the national government has put a wide variety of people to work. This project is designed to keep the sea from flooding the southwestern Netherlands. Engineers planned the construction of the dikes and dams. Biologists worked on the problems of preserving wildlife in the diked-off regions. Soil experts, construction workers, and many others were also put to work on the Delta Plan.

All these lawmakers and experts mean that more people work for the government in The Netherlands than in most other countries. Fifteen percent of all Nederlanders make their living in government work.

Nederlanders work at many other jobs besides manufacturing, farming, fishing, and government. Many have little shops and stores where they sell goods. Nederlanders also work as construction workers, bus and cab drivers, doctors, lawyers, teachers, and at just about every other profession and occupation you can name.

Chapter 7

THE PEOPLE AND THEIR CULTURE

The Netherlands is a small country. It is also one of the most crowded. It squeezes a population of over fourteen million into an area (land and water) of about 15,900 square miles (41,160 square kilometers). This means that an average of nearly one thousand persons live in each square mile of the country. By comparison, the United States has an average of sixty persons per square mile.

The people share many customs. Yet Nederlanders, like people everywhere, display a variety of regional and personal differences.

RELIGION

Once Dutch society was divided strictly according to religion. Protestants and Catholics often lived in separate parts of the community. They read separate newspapers, listened to separate radio stations, went to separate schools, and even played on separate sports teams. No law kept these two religious groups apart, nor did they fight with each other. They simply stayed separate from each other in daily life.

Today, the Catholics and the Protestants still attend separate churches. But many of the other barriers dividing these two religious groups have been broken. After working with each other in factories, living close together in the big cities, and fighting side by side during World War II, the Catholics and the Protestants are

Leidsestraat, a busy commercial street in Amsterdam

now more willing to deal with each other in their daily lives.

Now with a growing population of non-Christian residents, both followers of Islam and other religions, a new factor has been added to religious life in The Netherlands. The mosque is taking its place in many cities alongside the cathedral, church, and synagogue.

DRESS

Today, most of the Dutch dress the same as do people in much of the Western world. In the past, though, the Dutch had their own traditional clothes. The women wore long, colorful dresses and lace caps. The men wore baggy pants and round hats. Each province had its own style and colors. Anyone could tell which part of the country a woman came from just by looking at her cap. Now the Dutch wear traditional clothes in only a few villages. On holidays, however, many folks wear the old costumes to remind them of the days of their ancestors.

Inside a "klompen-maker's" shop in Marken

The most famous items of Dutch dress—wooden shoes—were first made long ago to protect Dutch feet from the wetness of the country. If you've ever walked through a puddle and come home with soaked feet, it's easy to figure out the benefits of wooden shoes, which keep your feet dry and warm. Like the other clothes, the wooden shoes were made in distinctive shapes and colors in various parts of the country. Some farmers, fishermen, gardeners, and street vendors still wear wooden shoes, which the Dutch call *klompen*. The *klompen* are not worn indoors. They are left outside, and regular leather shoes or slippers are put on for indoor use.

HOMES

Although millions of Nederlanders live in individual farmhouses and homes, millions of others live in apartment buildings. That's necessary in a country where space is so limited.

Flowers are found in window boxes and on houseboats throughout the Netherlands.

One unusual dwelling is the houseboat, many of which can be seen on the country's canals. Often they are old barges that have been remodeled as living quarters.

Regardless of the type of dwelling, Dutch homes are neat and clean. Nederlanders have long been famous for keeping their dwellings tidy. Many homes are decorated with flowers. Pretty flowers on a windowsill are considered as important as a colorful coat of paint on a wall to many Nederlanders.

FAMILY LIFE

"Your own hearth is worth gold," goes an old Dutch saying. That's the Nederlanders' way of saying that home and family are extremely important. If you traveled through The Netherlands and got to know the people, you'd find that the great majority of them feel that way.

Bicycles and mopeds are an important means of transportation.

Most Dutch families spend a great deal of time together. At the morning meal—often eggs, bread with cheese or ham, and tea—the family members ask each other how they slept. This kind of politeness and show of concern for others is taught to Dutch children at an early age. Parents also teach children other values, including respect for each person's individuality and the importance of freedom, cooperation, and fairness. These values, so often learned around the family table, have been reflected throughout the country's history.

After breakfast, the members of the family go off to their separate schools and jobs. Many travel by car, but quite a few who work and study near their homes ride bicycles. The country has thousands of miles of bike lanes to accommodate the millions of cyclists.

Many families who work or go to school close to home gather together for lunch. This is often just a sandwich.

In most homes a pot of tea steeping under the tea cozy and some cookies stand ready to welcome the children back from school. It provides *gezelligheid* (coziness) and creates a warm atmosphere for the children to share with mother the ups and downs of the school day.

The evening meal is usually big. It often starts with homemade soup, followed by a meat or fish dish and lots of vegetables. One famous Dutch dish is called *hutspot*, meaning *hodgepodge*. It's made of potatoes, carrots, and onions cooked with beef.

After dinner the family gathers together in one room to read and do homework. The Dutch are great readers. It was once figured that, on the average, Dutch men and women spend forty-five minutes per day just reading newspapers. This doesn't include time spent reading books. While the grown-ups are reading, the children are near at hand doing their homework. Homework is taken with an almost religious seriousness by the Dutch.

Dutch families often spend their weekends and days off together. They go to movies and to sporting events, and on nice days they bicycle out to the country or the beach. In the summer they drive off on family vacations. The Dutch spend so much time with their families that a visitor to the country once said, "The Dutch invented the family." What the Dutch look for, at home or when visiting friends, is *gezelligheid*, or a pleasant and cozy time. It is a quiet pleasure, perhaps just what is needed in a country where so many people live so near each other.

SPECIAL DAYS

For each member of a Dutch family, there is one day that is extra special. This is a person's birthday. Located prominently in a Dutch household is a calendar with every family member's birthday marked. On the happy day, the birthday person gets to stay in bed late. The family comes into the room to sing "Lang Zal Hij Leven" ("Long May He Live") if it's a male or "Lang Zal Zij Leven" ("Long May She Live") if it's a female. She or he receives presents and candies. Children celebrating their birthdays may even find their silverware decorated with little bows. At school or work, the birthday person is made to feel happy and important, and in return the birthday person may offer his classmates little cakes. In the evening, friends and relatives come over to celebrate.

Birthdays are considered so important that the Dutch send flowers and cards to far-flung relatives and friends on their birthdays. The queen's birthday is the most special of all. It is a national holiday. The Dutch flag is displayed that day throughout the country, parades are held, villagers carry flowers to the queen, and girls wear orange ribbons in their hair to honor the queen's family, the House of Orange.

The Nederlanders' respect for age is one reason why they pay so much attention to birthdays. To grow old in The Netherlands is considered an achievement. For the most part, senior citizens in The Netherlands are treated as important members of the community.

A birthday may be the most important day for an individual, but the Dutch have other days celebrated in common by the entire country. One of these is St. Nicholas Day, also known as *Sinterklaas* Day.

St. Nicholas was a bishop of the Catholic church long ago. He was known for giving gifts to the poor and for performing other good deeds. He became the patron saint of sailors and children. Because The Netherlands is a seafaring nation, its people built many churches to honor St. Nicholas. December 6, the day of his death, became a special holiday called *Sinterklaas* Day. On the eve before *Sinterklaas* Day, children received presents, and feasts were held.

Eventually, it became a custom for a man in each town to dress up in red and white bishop's robes and pretend to be St. Nicholas. He went from house to house, asked the children if they'd said their prayers and done their homework, and then gave them presents. When the Dutch settled in America, they brought the *Sinterklaas* tradition with them. But the children in America spoke the word *Sinterklaas* so quickly that the name soon was pronounced *Santa Claus*.

In The Netherlands today, there is no religious meaning to the *Sinterklaas* tradition. People of all religions celebrate the holiday. One special aspect to the gift giving is that a poem, often funny, is written to accompany each present. Also, presents are given anonymously.

St. Nicholas Day is fun. But Christmas in The Netherlands is a very solemn religious holiday. Nederlanders celebrate two days of Christmas—December 25 and 26. During the month before Christmas, farmers use long, thin hollow logs to perform the Midwinter Horn Blowing. It is a way to announce that Christmas is approaching. When Christmas finally arrives, people go to church and enjoy family get-togethers.

A week after Christmas comes a night of fun—New Year's Eve. At the stroke of midnight ships in the Dutch harbors blow their

Flower market in Utrecht

whistles, church bells are rung, and the sky is lighted brightly by fireworks.

It is quite possible to get as fat as Santa Claus during the winter holiday season. There are special foods for this time of year. There are *speculaas* (spicy cakes) and *borstplaat* (*Sinterklaas* candies) for *Sinterklaas* Day. There are *sneeuwballen* (whipped cream snowballs) and *oliebollen* (fruit-filled doughnuts) for New Year's Eve.

In the springtime, when the flowers are in bloom, there are flower festivals and parades throughout the land. During these festivals some Dutch towns look like giant flower shops.

The country also observes a very solemn day in the spring. This is Memorial Day, May 4, which commemorates the end of World War II. At precisely eight o'clock on the evening of May 4, everyone stops what he or she is doing. Cars and buses pull over to the side of the road. TV and radio shows are interrupted. This is

Secondary school in The Hague

the special time when Nederlanders remember their war dead and pray for peace in the future. The next day, May 5, is Liberation Day. This is a day of celebration. Street fairs, parades, and festivals are held in many communities.

EDUCATION

Children in The Netherlands must attend school from the age of six until the age of sixteen, or until they've completed ten years of school.

Most children start school long before their sixth birthdays. Almost 95 percent of all Dutch children go to nursery school from the age of four to six.

What the Dutch call primary education covers the ages of six to twelve. Dutch children learn reading, writing, arithmetic, and science. Language is also important to the young Nederlanders. Besides Dutch, many learn English, French, and German.

The Netherlands doesn't have a single basic four-year high school program. Instead, it has several varieties of four-, five-, and even six-year secondary education. Students who plan to attend a university have a choice of several kinds of secondary schools. Those who plan to go into business or industry can attend vocational secondary schools that prepare them for such jobs.

There are thirteen universities in The Netherlands. The oldest is the State University of Leiden, founded in 1575 by William the Silent. The University of Amsterdam, with about twenty thousand students, is the country's biggest university. Important to the improvement of farming methods is the Agricultural University of Wageningen, attended by about five thousand students.

THE ARTS

The Netherlands is world famous for its artists. The country has many art museums where people can view the works of Rembrandt, Hals, Vermeer, and van Gogh. The Rijksmuseum in Amsterdam is the country's most famous art museum, but there are many others.

The Concertgebouw Orchestra in Amsterdam is one of the finest symphony orchestras in the world. Other large cities in The Netherlands also have symphony orchestras.

Plays, ballets, and operas can be enjoyed in Dutch cities, too. Every summer there is a month-long festival in The Netherlands known as the Holland Festival. People from all over the world come to the country to enjoy concerts, operas, and plays performed by world famous artists.

The government of The Netherlands has programs to aid the country's not-so-famous artists. Painters and sculptors who can't

Frans Hals' painting, Officers and Soldiers of the Cloveniersdoelen *is shown at the Frans Hals Museum in Haarlem.*

earn a living by their art may sell their work to the government. These art works are then displayed in hospitals, schools, government buildings, and parks. The government also helps finance small magazines for writers and theater groups for actors.

The making of Delft pottery (left) and the cutting of diamonds (right) are important Dutch crafts.

CRAFTS

Long ago, the town of Delft became famous for producing fine white pottery decorated with blue designs. Today, Delft pottery is sold in stores in many countries.

For hundred of years, Amsterdam was famous for producing beautifully cut diamonds. Many of the diamond cutters were Jewish and were among those murdered by the German Nazis during World War II. In recent years the craft of diamond cutting has been revived.

For centuries, Dutch silversmiths have been famous for making silver jewelry, silverware, and other silver objects. The making of crystal glassware and pewter mugs and bowls are other crafts for which the Dutch are known.

Racing crew practicing in Delft

SPORTS

Nederlanders once played a game called Dutch pins. The object of the game was to knock over nine tall pins with a ball. The first person to get a score of exactly thirty-one was the winner. When the Dutch settled in what is now New York City, they brought this game with them. It evolved into the sport of bowling.

Today, the Dutch enjoy many sports. Soccer is one of the most popular. Many thousands of adults and young people play on the country's hundreds of soccer teams. In 1974 and 1978, Amsterdam's soccer team came in second in the World Cup soccer finals.

Other popular sports include bicycle riding, field hockey, gymnastics, volleyball, running, swimming, and sailing. There is an annual, four-day walking marathon near Nijmegen in which twenty thousand people participate. In the province of Friesland they play the sport of *fierljeppen*—pole-vaulting over canals.

When it gets very cold in the winter, the canals and rivers freeze. That makes almost every Dutch person happy. They get out their skates and glide down the rivers and canals. Sometimes schools close to allow the children to skate. If the ice gets thick enough, the "Eleven Towns Race" is held in Friesland. This is a 120-mile (193-kilometer) marathon skating race through eleven towns that are connected to each other by ice. Hockey is another popular winter sport in The Netherlands.

One interesting aspect of sports in The Netherlands is that everyone is encouraged to participate. There are teams for professionals and amateurs, men and women, young people and old people, and the physically handicapped.

LANGUAGE

Dutch is the national language of The Netherlands. It belongs to the Germanic family of languages, which also includes German and English.

There are various dialects in various parts of the country. It can be difficult for a person from one province to understand a person from another. In addition, the people in the province of Friesland have their own separate language, called Frisian. The Netherlands recognizes two official languages: Dutch and Frisian.

The Dutch used in the following words and phrases is the form understood by most Nederlanders.

SOME COMMON DUTCH WORDS

Moeder:	Mother	*Melk:*	Milk
Vader:	Father	*Koffie:*	Coffee
Zuster:	Sister	*Bier:*	Beer
Broer:	Brother	*Appel:*	Apple
Grootmoeder:	Grandmother	*Sinaasappel:*	Orange
Grootvader:	Grandfather	*Ja:*	Yes
Tante:	Aunt	*Nee:*	No
Oom:	Uncle	*Rechts:*	Right
Neef (M) Nicht (F):	Cousin	*Links:*	Left
Jongen:	Boy	*School:*	School
Meisje:	Girl	*Huiswerk:*	Homework
Man:	Man	*Kerk:*	Church
Vrouw:	Woman	*Leraar (male):*	Teacher
Ontbijt:	Breakfast	*Hoofd:*	Head
Lunch or Middageten:	Lunch	*Hand:*	Hand
Diner or Avondeten:	Dinner	*Arm:*	Arm
Keuken:	Kitchen	*Been:*	Leg
Badkamer:	Bathroom	*Vingers:*	Fingers
Huiskamer:	Living room	*Tenen:*	Toes
Mes:	Knife	*Klok:*	Clock
Vork:	Fork	*Automobiel:*	Automobile
Lepel:	Spoon	*Vliegtuig:*	Airplane
Eieren:	Eggs	*Dokter:*	Doctor
Pannekoeken:	Pancakes	*Verpleegster:*	Nurse
Kaas:	Cheese	*Advocaat:*	Lawyer
Sla:	Salad	*Dominee (Relig.):*	Pastor or Minister
Vlees:	Meat	*Minister (Political):*	Minister
Aardappelen:	Potatoes		

SOME DUTCH SAYINGS

Saying: Nu is Leiden in last
Translation: Now Leiden is in trouble
Meaning: We've got big problems

Saying: Je krijgt de wind van voren
Translation: You'll face the wind
Meaning: One day you'll have to pay the consequences for what you're doing

Madurodam, a miniature village, is on display in The Hague.

Saying: Je gooit je geld in het water
Translation: You're throwing your money into the water
Meaning: You're wasting your money

Saying: Een klap van de mallemolen gekregen
Translation: Hit by the mill
Meaning: Crazy

Saying: Ik roei met de riemen die ik heb
Translation: I'll row with the oars I have
Meaning: I'll make the best of the situation

Saying: Gods molens malen langzaam
Translation: God's mills grind slowly but surely
Meaning: God does things in His own good time

Saying: Eigen haard is goud waard
Translation: Your own hearth is worth gold
Meaning: There's nothing as good as family and home

Saying: Dit zet geen zoden aan de dijk
Translation: This puts no sod on the dike
Meaning: This is a colossal waste of time

Saying: Aan de dijk gezet
Translation: Kicked out onto the dike
Meaning: Fired from a job

Chapter 8
SOME FAMOUS
NEDERLANDERS

REMBRANDT (1606-1669)

Hieronymus Bosch, Jan Vermeer, Frans Hals, Jacob van Ruisdael, Pieter de Hooch, Vincent van Gogh, Rembrandt—these are great names in The Netherlands' gallery of artists. By far the greatest of them all was Rembrandt, who was born in Leiden and whose full name was Rembrandt Harmenszoon van Rijn.

As a boy, Rembrandt drew pictures of windmills, cloudy skies, and his sister. As a young man, he became famous for his portraits. He painted portraits of his mother reading and of his father dressed up in unusual costumes. He also did portraits of beggars and others whom he met on the streets of Leiden. The word spread: Rembrandt could capture on canvas the essence of a person.

The young artist went to Amsterdam, where the wealthiest citizens soon were knocking at his door. In this time before the invention of the photographic camera, people wanted to have their portraits painted. Rembrandt became the most famous portrait artist in Amsterdam. He captured details of people's expressions that revealed their personalities. He was so wondrous at painting light and shadow that his pictures seemed to glow.

Rembrandt's The Night Watch

Rembrandt created other paintings besides the ones he was paid for. He did seven of his wife, Saskia. One, *Rembrandt and Saskia,* shows the happy young artist with his wife sitting on his lap. He did portraits of his son, Titus, which give you a feeling of Rembrandt's love for his boy. As the mood struck him, Rembrandt also painted animals and landscapes. He bought a house in the Jewish section of Amsterdam to be near the descendants of Old Testament figures. Then he used his neighbors' faces as models for great Biblical paintings.

Everything went wrong in Rembrandt's personal life. Although Saskia and he had four children, only Titus lived past infancy. Then in 1642 Saskia died. To add to his woes, Rembrandt was short of money. He had spent a fortune on works of art to decorate his house. He had also been spending much of his time painting for his own pleasure rather than on works for which he was paid. A painting he *was* paid for, *The Night Watch,* was a disappointment to the soldiers who had commissioned it. The faces of some of them were almost lost in shadows. Today *The Night Watch* is considered one of the world's great paintings. But in Rembrandt's time it was hung in a dark corner of a building. After this episode, Rembrandt's reputation as a portrait painter ebbed.

Rembrandt's misfortunes seemed to deepen his understanding of people. Towards the end of his life he created some of his greatest works. He did *David Playing the Harp Before Saul* in 1658, and in 1669, shortly after the death of Titus, he did a wonderful self-portrait. A few months later, Rembrandt died.

Only a few members of his family attended Rembrandt's funeral. A lawyer looking over his possessions found a few canvasses, a Bible, and some clothes. Scattered about the world, though, were 600 paintings, 1,400 drawings, and 300 etchings he had created.

As the years passed, people realized the greatness of these works. Today, "Rembrandts" that once hung in dark corners are worth millions of dollars and Rembrandt is remembered as one of the supremely great artists of all time.

FRANS HALS (1580? — 1666)

Frans Hals is usually considered the country's second greatest artist. He lived most of his life in the town of Haarlem, The Netherlands.

Much is known of Frans Hals from court records. He drank too much liquor, squandered his money, and got into all kinds of trouble. Yet throughout his long life he painted hundreds of great portraits.

Hals did many portraits of wealthy people. These portraits, for which he was paid handsomely, show people dressed in fancy

Singing Boy with Flute
by Frans Hals

clothes and jewelry. Hals also did paintings for his own enjoyment. He liked to do portraits of people he met in taverns. The persons in these paintings are usually happy and twinkly eyed. They are often shown raising a glass of wine or playing a musical instrument. *The Merry Lute Player* is one such painting. There is so much joy in these paintings that people who look at them in museums often break out into big grins.

The father of at least a dozen children, Hals took special joy in portraying children. One famous painting, *The Rommelpot Player*, shows a group of children laughing as they listen to a man beating on a drum.

The town of Haarlem was proud of Frans Hals. Books were written about him and his works were hung in the Town Hall and in many homes. When Hals reached his eighties, he was so poor that he couldn't even pay the baker's bill. The people of Haarlem gave Hals money and the job of restoring old paintings. Hals died at the age of eighty-six and was buried in the Haarlem cathedral. Many of his portraits can be seen in his hometown of Haarlem and in Amsterdam.

Anton van Leeuwenhoek

ANTON VAN LEEUWENHOEK (1632-1723)

Anton van Leeuwenhoek, born in Delft, was an unlikely figure
to become a great scientist. His education was meager. He earned
his living at a dry goods store where he sold cloth and other items
to the people of Delft.

To determine the quality of his cloth, Leeuwenhoek used a
magnifying glass. He enjoyed the magnifying glass so much that
he examined coins, buttons, and other objects with it. Then,
starting in about 1660, Leeuwenhoek began making microscopes.
He carefully ground the glass himself. The first microscope had
been invented in 1590 by another Nederlander, Zacharias Janssen.
But Leeuwenhoek made microscopes that were better than any
built before. They could magnify objects 275 times.

By day Leeuwenhoek continued to work in his store. But by
night he pursued his hobby of making microscopes and looking
through them. Leeuwenhoek made many discoveries. He looked
at a drop of water and observed thousands of tiny organisms
swimming about in it. These were bacteria and protozoa. In the
diary where he recorded his observations Leeuwenhoek called the
small organisms "animalcules," "wee animals," and "wretched
beasties."

Leeuwenhoek's curiosity about the world of little things was tremendous. He caught bees and studied their legs, mouths, eyes, and stingers. He caught houseflies and looked at their brains, eyes, and legs. He caught cockroaches and observed their blood. He also observed fleas, lice, skin, hairs, human blood, seeds, and spermatozoa.

In one interesting episode, Leeuwenhoek went days without brushing his teeth just to observe the bacteria that grew inside his mouth. Of this he wrote: "All the people living in our United Netherlands are not as many as the living animals that I carry in my own mouth this very day."

Leuwenhoek did not understand the relationship between bacteria and disease. But he was the first scientist to observe bacteria and other forms of microscopic life. Because of his discoveries of very small forms of life, Leeuwenhoek is called the "Father of Microbiology." This great self-taught scientist was still studying blood and the eyes of flies past the age of ninety.

CHRISTIAAN HUYGENS (1629-1695)

Christiaan Huygens was born in The Hague. At a young age he learned many languages and played several musical instruments. At sixteen he enrolled at the University of Leiden. Huygens became a brilliant astronomer, mathematician, and inventor.

In the early 1600s the astronomer Galileo had noted the peculiar shape of the planet Saturn. Astronomers wondered about that weird shape, but their telescopes were too weak to reveal its cause. Christiaan Huygens was intrigued by Saturn. He built powerful telescopes to view it better. In 1655 he made a startling discovery—Saturn has rings. That same year he discovered Titan,

Desiderius Erasmus (far left) and Christiaan Huygens (left) were two great Dutch scholars.

the ringed planet's largest moon. Some of the telescopes built by Huygens were more than 30 feet (9 meters) long.

Huygens applied his brilliant mind to other fields. In 1657 he invented the pendulum clock to help sailors determine their position at sea. The micrometer—used to measure very short distances—was another of his inventions. Christiaan Huygens applied his great mathematical genius to help us in our modern understanding of light, gravity, movement, and other scientific subjects.

DESIDERIUS ERASMUS (1466?-1536)

Desiderius Erasmus was born in Rotterdam. He became a priest who was both a religious man and a great thinker. Erasmus was a humanist—he thought that each human being, be he a king or a poor farmer, has great individual importance.

In his books Erasmus said that priests should teach people the meaning of the Bible, rather than just concentrate on religious ceremonies. He condemned war, insisted that people should be kind to one another, and asserted that every person has the ability to understand the basic ideas of Christianity. Erasmus also published new editions of the New Testament.

*Baruch Spinoza
was a philosopher.*

BARUCH SPINOZA (1632-1677)

Is there a God? What is the place of human beings in the universe? How can people be happy? These are a few of the questions pondered by thinkers called philosophers. One of the greatest philosophers ever was Baruch Spinoza, born in Amsterdam.

Spinoza's family, which was Jewish, had come to The Netherlands for religious freedom. From an early age, Spinoza thought for himself. The Jewish community threw him out of their congregation because he questioned their beliefs. Spinoza was offered a job as a professor. He turned it down because he wanted to pursue what he called "freedom of philosophizing" without having to please an employer. For a living, Spinoza ground lenses in The Hague. He wrote philosophy books in his spare time.

Spinoza believed in the power of the human mind. He thought that the individual could understand the universe through thought. His own conclusion was that every single thing in the universe is a part of God. Spinoza said that the happy person is one who understands that he or she is a part of God.

*Self-portrait by
Vincent van Gogh*

VINCENT VAN GOGH (1853-1890)

Experts now consider Vincent van Gogh the greatest Dutch artist since the Golden Age. But in his lifetime, van Gogh was considered a failure at everything he did, including painting.

Vincent was born in 1853 in the town of Groot-Zundert. As a young man, he had a job in his uncle's art gallery. Because Vincent was loud and argued with the customers, he was fired. He decided to become a minister, but couldn't pass the tests. Because of his desire to help the poor, Vincent became a missionary to coal miners in Belgium. He dressed in rags, lived in a shack, and shared his food with the miners. When other missionaries came to visit, they didn't like the fact that Vincent was living in such poverty. Again, he was fired.

Ashamed to return home, Vincent roamed the countryside alone. He slept outside beneath the stars. During this period he did some sketches. He sent them to his brother Theo, who gave Vincent money to help him paint.

The Vincent van Gogh Museum in Amsterdam

Vincent continued to draw and paint while he moved about to Brussels, The Hague, Antwerp, and Paris. Often he didn't have a bed to sleep in or food to eat. He spent his money on art supplies. In these early years of his career he painted pictures of the poor people whom he met on his travels.

In 1888 Vincent moved to the town of Arles in southern France. There he did some of his best paintings. His pictures of haystacks and sailboats, wheat fields and sunflowers, often were signed with the single name "Vincent." Van Gogh was brilliant in his use of bright colors. He also had the ability to project his own feelings into his pictures. He could make a haystack seem happy, a cafe look sad, and a starry sky appear terrifying.

In van Gogh's entire lifetime, only one of his paintings was sold—and that was through his brother Theo's efforts. Vincent also had severe personal problems. He suffered from epilepsy, a disorder that caused him to have violent seizures. At the time people didn't understand epilepsy, and so he was considered to be "crazy." Sick, poor, and a failure in just about every aspect of his life, Vincent van Gogh killed himself at the age of thirty-seven. Much too late for Vincent, he was later recognized as one of the greatest and most original artists of modern times.

ANNE FRANK (1929-1945)

Anne Frank was born in Frankfurt, Germany. Her family was Jewish. When Anne was little, the German Nazis began to threaten Jews. Anne, her sister, and their parents fled to The Netherlands. But in 1940, during World War II, the Germans invaded The Netherlands. By now the German Nazis were murdering Jews. To save their lives, Anne Frank and her family hid in a secret section of a building with four other people.

Friends brought them food. To pass the time, Anne and the seven others in the attic read, wrote, and listened to the radio. They had to be quiet when others were in the building. If the Germans discovered them, it meant death.

Anne wrote about her thoughts and feelings in a diary she'd been given on her thirteenth birthday. She described her feelings about growing up, her arguments and talks with her parents, and her hopes for the future. As the months passed, she told of falling in love with a young man who was also hiding in the attic. She also decided to be a writer when she grew up.

She never got the chance. After more than three years of hiding, Anne and the others were discovered. They were sent to concentration camps. In 1945—a few months before her sixteenth birthday—Anne died in a camp. But her diary was found and later published as a book called *The Diary of a Young Girl.*

The Diary of a Young Girl is now famous. It helps people understand the humanity and individuality of just one victim of World War II. After reading it, people realize that each of the war's millions of victims was an individual, just as Anne Frank was. In this way her diary keeps alive the horrors of World War II to generations born long after the war ended.

Queen Wilhelmina (left) and former Queen Juliana (right)

QUEEN WILHELMINA (1880-1962)

Wilhelmina was born in The Hague. When she was just ten years old, she became queen of The Netherlands. Because Wilhelmina was so young, her mother ruled for her until she was eighteen years old.

Queen Wilhelmina, known for her strength, courage, and determination, helped guide the country through two world wars. When the Germans tried to capture her during World War II, she escaped to London. From there she directed Netherlands' troops against the enemy. In 1948 Queen Wilhelmina gave up the throne to her daughter Juliana. At the age of seventy-three, Wilhelmina helped in the relief efforts after the 1953 flood.

QUEEN JULIANA (1909-   )

Queen Juliana was known for her down-to-earth style. Upon becoming monarch in 1948 she said, "For a queen the task of being a mother is just as important as it is for every other Netherlands woman." She drove her children to school herself, sometimes stopping to pick up other children.

In her public life, Queen Juliana promoted programs to help poor people, old people, and children throughout the world. In 1980, on her seventy-first birthday, Queen Juliana gave up the throne to her daughter Beatrix.

QUEEN BEATRIX (1938-   )

Beatrix Wilhelmina Armgard was born at the Soestdijk Palace in the town of Baarn. During World War II Beatrix was sent to Canada, where she lived for five years and went to school.

At the end of the war the royal family was reunited in The Netherlands. Beatrix was given an education to prepare her for becoming queen. She went to the University of Leiden, founded four centuries earlier by her ancestor, William the Silent. She rode her bicycle to class with the other students and enjoyed sailing, horseback riding, and other sports. In her studies she concentrated on law, history, and world affairs. Beatrix earned the doctorate of law degree from the university.

In 1980 Beatrix's mother, Queen Juliana, gave up the throne. In a ceremony at the Nieuw Kerk (New Church) in Amsterdam, Beatrix was inaugurated as queen. Beatrix and her husband, Prince Claus, have three sons. The firstborn, Prince Willem-Alexander, will one day become king of The Netherlands.

Heavy mists often cover the land, giving the familiar landmarks a mysterious look.

Chapter 9

MYTHS OF THE NETHERLANDS

You can learn a lot about a people from the myths and legends they have told over the centuries. Dutch tales abound with mermaids, floods, pirates, cruel rich people, and devils who offer riches to the poor in exchange for their souls. Following are three of the many tales told by Nederlanders.

THE RICH WOMAN OF STAVOREN

The town of Stavoren is in the province of Friesland. Once Stavoren was a wealthy port city. Today it is just a little town. One of the factors that led to its downfall was a sandbar that formed at the entrance to the Stavoren harbor. Ships could no longer enter the harbor. This sandbar is called *Het Vrouwezand* (The Woman's Sand), and the people of the region tell a tale of how it got there.

Long ago, the story begins, there was a widow known as The Lady of Stavoren. She was the wealthiest person in Stavoren and possibly the wealthiest person in the entire world. Her treasure chests were filled with gold, rubies, pearls, and other riches. She owned dozens of ships. Her clothes were fit for a queen and her house was like a palace. But The Lady of Stavoren was very stingy. If anyone asked for help, she was sure to say, "No!"

Despite her riches, The Lady of Stavoren was unsatisfied. She wanted more. Finally she realized that what she really wanted was *the* most precious object in all the world. She had no idea what that might be, but she ordered her best sea captain to find it. "Sail seven times around the seven seas if you have to, Captain," she ordered, "but bring me back the most precious thing in all the world. The ship is filled with gold to pay for the treasure you find. If you don't succeed, a most sad fate awaits you."

Seeing that he had no choice, the captain sailed away from Stavoren. Over the years, he stopped at many ports. He saw jewels, precious fabrics, and other treasures. But The Lady of Stavoren had all of these. In the seventh year of his voyage he came to a port city where he found the usual treasures of gold, silver, and jewels. The captain was just about to give up and return empty-handed to The Lady when he noticed a crowd around an old man in the town square.

"This is the most precious thing on earth," said the old man, holding up something that gleamed golden in the sunlight.

"What is it?" shouted the excited sea captain.

"Kernels of wheat—God's gift to people," said the old man. "Plant them and you can grow fields of wheat. From the wheat, bread can be made to feed people."

"How simple and true! Wheat must be the greatest treasure on earth," said the captain, buying some.

When the captain returned to Stavoren, a crowd was waiting at the harbor. "What did you bring me after all these years, Captain?" asked the greedy Lady.

"Wheat, my lady," said the captain, holding up the golden grains. "A wise man told me that it's far more valuable than gold, because it can feed the hungry."

The Lady of Stavoren couldn't have cared less about feeding the hungry. "All these years of searching and this is what you bring me!" she screamed. "You and your crew dump that wheat into the water!"

Before the wheat could be thrown overboard, an old beggar in the crowd said, "Wait! If you waste God's gift of wheat, Lady, you'll wind up a beggar in search of bread yourself. And you—the people of Stavoren who know better—if you don't stop her from doing this you'll be sorry, too."

"*I* a beggar?" the enraged Lady shrieked. She pulled a diamond ring from her finger and hurled it into the sea. "That's as likely as that ring coming back to me!"

Although the people of Stavoren knew better, they laughed at the old beggar who had said The Lady would wind up a beggar someday. "The Lady wind up poor!" they jeered, as the wheat was dumped into the ocean. The townspeople prepared to drive the old beggar out of town, but he mysteriously disappeared as soon as the wheat hit the water.

The Lady still craved the greatest treasure on earth. After firing the captain, she loaded all her gold and riches onto her vast fleet and sent every last ship to sea. "One of you is bound to find the greatest treasure on earth," she told her sea captains. "Whoever succeeds will be handsomely rewarded."

A few days after she'd sent out her fleet, The Lady gave a banquet. A large fish was one of the delicacies. As this fish was cut open, The Lady and her guests noticed something glittering inside it. "The diamond ring—it's come back from the sea!" gasped the guests.

After that, disaster struck. A hurricane sank every last one of The Lady's ships. Floods ruined her lovely home and warehouses.

As things went from bad to worse, she had to sell her jewels, her furniture, and finally even her house. She wandered the streets, begging for crusts of bread.

Over the years a sandbar formed at the harbor entrance, blocking ships from entering. This was the townspeople's punishment for making fun of the old beggar. On the sandbar some of the wheat dumped in the ocean took root. The sandbar and the tall grassy weeds that look like wheat can still be seen. They are all that remain of The Lady of Stavoren's treasures.

SYTSKE FOOLS THE DEVIL

Many Dutch tales tell of Joost and his evil tricks. Joost was probably the wickedest devil in hell. He was forever trying to obtain a more important position in hell by tricking people out of their souls. It was the misfortune of a young Friesland farmer named Jelle to become the target of Joost and his evil tricks.

Jelle and his wife, Sytske, were very poor. They didn't have much to eat. But even worse was that their barn was falling apart. This meant that their few farm animals had no protection from the weather. One day Jelle walked to town and asked a rich man for a loan. The man turned him down. Jelle was very sad as he walked back to his old, run-down farm.

On the road home, Jelle became aware of someone following him. When Jelle turned around he saw a handsome man, dressed in black, smiling at him. "Don't be afraid, I want to help you," said the man in black. "What is your trouble?"

Jelle was quite scared, because the man's eyes glowed strangely. But he answered, "My barn is falling apart and Sytske and I don't have money to fix it."

"A small problem!" said the stranger, who, of course, was really the devil Joost. "I'll have my assistants build a new barn for you. You only have to give me your soul in return. And I won't collect it until the end of your life."

Jelle really knew better than to give up his soul, but he was in such dire straits that he was tempted to go against his own judgment. To tempt him further, Joost added that if the barn wasn't finished before the first crowing of the roosters, Jelle wouldn't have to give up his soul.

Still knowing that it was very wrong, Jelle agreed. When he got home to his wife, he couldn't look her in the eye. They ate their cabbage soup and sour-apple pancakes in silence. When Sytske asked her young husband what was wrong, he didn't answer.

That night both Jelle and Sytske heard hammering and sawing out at the barn. "It's just the wind," Jelle lied, but his wife got out of bed and looked out the window. There were Joost's assistant devils at work on the new barn. With their horns, wings, and sharp claws, they were quite ugly. "Jelle, tell me what's going on!" Sytske demanded. No longer able to keep his secret, Jelle told Sytske how he'd exchanged his soul for a brand-new barn.

"Your soul for a barn! Have you been hit by the mill, man?" she yelled. "Well, Joost won't get *my* husband's soul—ever."

"It's no use," said Jelle. "Joost said the only way I can keep my soul is if they don't finish the barn before the first crowing of the roosters. I'm sure they'll finish, because there are hours before daybreak when the roosters always crow."

The brave Sytske was willing to face all the devils in hell to save her husband's soul. She also had an idea. Quietly she went out to the barn, which was now almost finished. She was so quiet that not even the roosters noticed her enter the barn. Suddenly Sytske opened her mouth and crowed, in her best imitation of a rooster: "Cock-a-doodle-DOO!" The roosters awoke. Thinking it was dawn, they, too, began to crow!

As Jelle ran out to join his wife in the barn, he saw the angry demons flying away. You can imagine how angry Joost was to learn that the roosters—and he—had been fooled by Sytske.

The young couple had to put the finishing touches on the new barn. As for Jelle, he realized that, no matter how poor a person is, it's bad business to trade one's soul for a new barn.

THE MERMAID WHO LIVED LIKE A PERSON

In the province of North Holland, they tell a mermaid story. Long ago, they say, a terrible storm broke the dike near Edam. Seawater flowed into Purmer Lake. Along with the fish that were washed in beyond the dike, there was a mermaid. The dike was repaired before the mermaid could get back out to sea, so she was trapped in Purmer Lake.

Every morning several young milkmaids took a boat across Purmer Lake to get to the cow pasture. One morning these young girls heard sad singing as they crossed the lake. The next morning they saw that it was a mermaid singing the sad song. Over the next few days the girls offered the mermaid food and talked sweetly to her. Each day she swam closer to the girls. One day, when she swam very close to their boat, the milkmaids grabbed her and pulled her aboard. Then they rowed back to Edam.

The people of Edam were kind to the mermaid. Once they saw that she was willing to stay with them, they gave her clothes and taught her the Dutch language. They even built her a little

Keukenhof Gardens in Lisse

house, which must have had a good-sized bathtub to accommodate her need for water! When the townspeople of nearby Haarlem heard of the wondrous mermaid who lived like a human, they asked her to come live with them. In Haarlem they built a huge house for her, staffed with servants. She made many friends in Haarlem and lived a happy and long life. Her funeral was attended by hundreds of people and the burgomaster of Haarlem gave a lovely speech in her memory.

When children heard their parents tell this story, they got the message: Be kind to everyone. If you ever visit The Netherlands, you'll find that the people *are* kind and considerate. You'll also find that the land of dikes, windmills, tulips, and wooden shoes is one of the most beautiful and interesting countries on earth.

Cities and towns in the Netherlands.

Name	Ref
Aalsmeer	B4
Aalten	C6
Alkmaar	B4
Almelo	B6
Alphen aan den Rijn	B4
Ameland, island	A5
Amersfoort	B5
Amsterdam	B4
Anjum	A6
Apeldoorn	B5
Appingedam	A6
Arnhem	C5
Assen	B6
Asten	C5
Axel	C3
Baarn	B5
Barneveld	B5
Beek	D5
Beemster, polder (1612)	B4
Bergen aan Zee	B4
Bergen op Zoom	C4
Beveland, North, island	C3
Beveland, South, island	C3
Beverwijk	B4
Blija	A5
Bolsward	A5
Borculo	B6
Borger	B6
Borne	B6
Boxmeer	C5
Boxtel	C5
Brabant, North, province	C4 & C5
Breda	C4
Breskens	C3
Buitenpost	A6
Bussum	B5
Coevorden	B6
Colijnsplaat	C3
De Cocksdorp	A4
Dedemsvaart	B6
Delft	B4
Delfzijl	A6
Den Burg	A4
Den Helder	B4
Den Hoorn	A4
Den Oever	B5
Deventer	B6
Diever	B6
Doetinchem	C6
Dokkum	A5
Domburg	C3
Dommel, river	C5
Dordrecht	C4
Drachten	A6
Drenthe, province	B6
East Flevoland (1957), polder	B5
Echt	C5
Edam	B5
Ede	B5
Egmond aan Zee	B4
Eindhoven	C5
Elburg	B5
Emmen	B6
Enkhuizen	B5
Enschede	B6
Epe	B5
Ermelo	B5
Flevoland, East (1957), polder	B5
Flevoland, South (1968), polder	B5
Franeker	A5
Friesland, province	A5 & A6
Gelderland, province	B5
Geldermalsen	C5
Geldrop	C5
Geleen	D5
Gemert	C5
Gennep	C5
Goeree, island	C3 & C4
Goes	C3
Goor	B6
Gorinchem	C5
Gouda	B4
Goudswaard	C4
Groenlo	B6
Groningen	A6
Groningen, province	A6
Haaksbergen	B6
Haamstede	C3
Haarlem	B4
Haarlemmermeer	B4
Hardenberg	B6
Harderwijk	B5
Haren	A6
Harlingen	A5
Hasselt	B6
Hattem	B6
Heerde	B6
Heerenveen	B5
Heerlen	D5
Helmond	C5
Hengelo	B6
Hillegom	B4
Hilversum	B5
Hoek van Holland	C4
Hoensbroek	D5
Holland, North, province	B4
Holland, South, province	B4
Hollum	A5
Hoogeveen	B6
Hoogezand	A6
Hoorn	B5
Huizen	B5
Hulst	C4
Hunse, river	A6
IJmuiden	B4
IJssel, river	B6
IJssellakepolders, Southern, province	B5
IJsselmeer (Zuider Zee), lake	B5
Kampen	B5
Katwijk aan Zee	B4
Kerkrade	D6
Lauwers Zee, bay and river	A6
Leeuwarden	A5
Leiden	B4
Lek, river	C4
Lemelerveld	B6
Lemmer	B5
Limburg, province	D5
Lochem	B6
Luidhorn	A6
Maas, river	C5
Maastricht	D5
Makkinga	B6
Makkum	A5
Marken, island	B5
Markerwaard, polder	B5
Medemblik	B5
Meppel	B6
Middelburg	C3
Middelharnis	C4
Monnikendam	B5
Neder Rijn (Lower Rhine), river	C5
Nes	A5
Nieuweroord	B6
Nijkerk	B5
Nijmegen	C5
Noordwijk-Binnen	B4
North Beveland, island	C3
North Brabant, province	C5
North Holland, province	B4
North Sea	A2, A3, B2, B3
Northeast Polder (1942)	B5
Northwest Polder (1930)	B5
Oldenzaal	B6
Olst	B6
Ommen	B6
Ooltgensplaat	C4
Oostburg	C3
Oosterend	A4
Oosterend	A5
Oosterhout	C4
Oostmahorn	A6
Oost-Vlieland	A5
Oostvoorne	C4
Oss	C5
Ouddorp	C3
Oude-Pekela	A7
Overflakkee, island	C4
Overijssel, province	B6
Purmerend	B4
Putte	C4
Raalte	B6
Rheden	B6
Rhenen	C5
Rhine River (Neder Rijn)	C5
Rhine River (Old Rhine)	B4
Rijssen	B6
Rijswijk	B4
Roermond	C5
Roodeschool	A6
Roosendaal	C4
Rotterdam	C4
Rottumeroog, island	A6
Sappemeer	A6
Schagen	B4
Scheveningen	B4
Schiedam	C4
Schiermonnikoog, island	A6
Schoonhoven	C4
Schouwen, island	C3
's Hertogenbosch	C5
Sint Jacobinparochie	A5
Sittard	D5
Sneek	A5
South Beveland, island	C3
South Holland, province	B4
Southern IJssellakepolders, province	B5
Stadskanaal	A6
Stavenisse	C4
Stavoren	B5
Steenbergen	C4
Steenwijk	B6
Tegelen	C6
Ter Apel	B6
Terneuzen	C3
Terschelling, island	A5
Texel, island	A4
The Hague ('s Gravenhage)	B4
Tholen	C4
Tiel	C5
Tilburg	C5
Tjeukemeer, lake	B5
Uden	C5
Uithuizen	B5
Urk	B5
Utrecht	B5
Utrecht, province	B5
Vaals	D5
Vaalserberg, mountain	D5
Valkenswaard	C5
Vechte, river	B6
Veendam	A6
Velsen	B4
Venlo	C6
Vianen	C5
Vlaardingen	C4
Vlieland, island	A4 & A5
Vlissingen	C3
Waal, river	C5 & C6
Waalwijk	C5
Wadden Zee	A5
Wageningen	C5
Walcheren, island	C3
Wassenaar	B4
Weert	C5
Weesp	B5
West Frisian Islands	A4, A5, A6
Westkapelle	C3
Westerschelde, channel	C3
West-Terschelling	A5
Wieringermeer (1930), polder	B5
Wijhe	B6
Wildervank	A6
Willemstad	C4
Winschoten	A7
Winsum	A6
Winterswijk	C6
Woerden	B4
Workum	B5
Wormerveer	B4
Yerseke	C4
Zaandam	B4
Zaltbommel	C5
Zandvoort	B4
Zeeland, province	C3
Zeist	B5
Zevenaar	C6
Zierikzee	C3
Zoutkamp	A6
Zutphen	B6
Zwartsluis	B6
Zwolle	B6

MINI-FACTS AT A GLANCE

GENERAL INFORMATION

Official Name: The Netherlands. This means "lowlands."

Other names: The Netherlands is also called Holland. In 1581 it was known as The Dutch Republic. When the French ruled The Netherlands (1795-1813), they called it the Batavian Republic.

Capital: Amsterdam

Seat of Government: The Hague

Official Language: Dutch, Frisian

Other Languages: Many people also speak German, English, and Flemish. (Flemish is essentially the same as Dutch.) People who live in the province of Friesland speak Frisian.

Government: The Netherlands is part of the Kingdom of the Netherlands, which also includes the Netherlands Antilles islands in the Caribbean Sea. The Netherlands is a constitutional monarchy. This means the government is based on a constitution and the ruler is a monarch—a queen or king. The monarch is head of state but rules through the government and parliament. Queens and kings are not crowned in the Netherlands, but take an oath of allegiance to the constitution.

The country is governed by a prime minister and cabinet ministers. The prime minister, appointed by the ruler, chooses a cabinet. Parliament consists of the First Chamber and the Second Chamber. Both chambers can pass laws but only members of the Second Chamber can propose or amend laws. The 75-member First Chamber is elected by the provincial lawmakers to six-year terms. The people directly elect the 150-member Second Chamber to four-year terms. Each of the eleven provinces is governed by its own commissioner appointed by the monarch. Every city and town has a chief official called a burgomaster also appointed by the monarch. Each polder—or set of polders—is run by a waterschap council. All citizens who are eighteen years old or older may vote.

Flag: The flag is composed of three stripes colored red, white, and blue. Before 1630 an orange stripe instead of a red stripe was at the top.

Coat of Arms: Symbols of the Dutch royal family are shown on the coat of arms. Arrows and a sword stand for strength through unity.

National Song: "Wilhelmus van Nassouwe" ("William of Nassau")

Religion: The Netherlands has religious freedom. About 30 percent of the people are Protestant. About 30 percent are Catholic. Approximately thirty thousand Jews live in the Netherlands. About 30 percent do not belong to any church. In the past Protestants and Catholics stayed separate from each other. Today they still attend separate churches, but the barriers dividing these groups have broken down.

Money: Guilders and cents. One hundred cents equal one guilder. Paper bills are issued in denominations of 5, 10, 20, 50, 100, 500, and 1,000 guilders. Coins are 5, 10, and 25 cents and 1 and 2.5 guilders.

Weights and Measures: The Netherlands uses the metric system.

Population: 14,300, 000 (1982 estimate). Eighty-six percent of the people live in cities. The Netherlands has one of the highest population densities in the world.

Provinces: Thirty-eight percent of the people live in the two coastal provinces of North Holland and South Holland.

Drenthe	423,600
Friesland	592,400
Gelderland	1,719,100
Groningen	559,100
Limburg	1,077,200
North Brabant	2,085,400
North Holland	2,312,300
Overijssel	1,033,800
South Holland	3,121,500
Utrecht	916,700
Zeeland	353,700

Cities: Seventeen cities have populations over 100,000·

Amsterdam	700,759
Apeldoorn	142,367
Arnhem	129,160
Breda	117,754
Dordrecht	108,576
Eindhoven	195,599
Enschede	144,590
Groningen	165,146
Haarlem	156,025
The Hague	454,300
Leiden	103,457
Maastricht	111,487
Nijmegen	147,172
Rotterdam	568,167
Tilburg	153,957
Utrecht	234,543
Zaandam	129,864

(Population based on 1982 figures from Central Bureau for Statistics, Ministry of Economic Affairs, The Netherlands.

GEOGRAPHY

Land Regions: The Netherlands has four land regions. The Dunes region is located along the North Sea coast of The Netherlands and includes the West Frisian Islands. Very little can grow here, but the region is useful because it holds the sea in place. The Polders (region) is below sea level. The region is rich farmland. The Netherlands' largest cities are located in the Polders. The Sand Plains region is about 100 ft. (30 m) above sea level. The soil is dry but irrigation ditches bring water to farms. Fruit is grown in the fertile soils of the Southern Uplands. This is the highest region.

Highest Point: Vaalser Berg, located in the Southern Uplands, 1,057 ft. (322 m)

Lowest Point: Prins Alexander Polder, 22 ft. (6.7 m) below sea level

Rivers: The Rhine and the Maas are two major rivers that flow through The Netherlands. Other rivers include the Waal, the Lek, the IJssel, the Rotte, the Amstel, the Neder Rijn and the Westerschelde.

Mountains: The Netherlands has no mountains.

Polders: The Netherlands has four large polders—Wieringermeer Polder, Northeast Polder, Eastern Flevoland, and Southern Flevoland. The Markerwaard, which is still under construction, if completed would be a fifth polder. More than two fifths of The Netherlands consists of polders.

Climate: The climate is mild and damp throughout The Netherlands. Summer temperatures are usually in the 60s F. (10 C.). Winter temperatures are usually in the 30s F. (-1 C.). Skies are often cloudy. Rainfall is about 30 in. (76 cm) per year.

Greatest Distance: North to South, about 196 mi. (315 km).
East to West, about 167 mi. (269 km)

Coastline: 228 mi. (367 km)

Area: 15,892 sq. mi. (41,160 km²)

NATURE

Trees: Only about 8 percent of The Netherlands has trees. Common trees are beech, oak, and pine.

Birds: The Netherlands has no distinctive birds. Birds are similar to those in other Western European countries. Sea gulls appear in coastal areas.

Animals: The Netherlands has almost no large or wild animals aside from wild boar and deer within The Hague Veluwe Park in central Netherlands.

Fish: Common fish include herring, flatfish, and haddock.

EVERYDAY LIFE

Food: Typical breakfast might include eggs, bread, cheese, ham, and tea. Lunch is usually a sandwich. Dinner might include soup, fish or meat, and vegetables.

Clothes: Most people dress the same way people in North America do. Traditional clothing is still worn by some people in the Zeeland and West Frisian Islands. Women wear long skirts or dresses and lace caps. Men wear baggy pants and round caps. Wooden shoes are commonly worn by people such as farmers or fishermen who work outdoors.

Homes: Because The Netherlands is a crowded country, houses are small. The Dutch keep their houses neat and decorate them with flowers.

What People Do for a Living: Manufacturing and mining, 24 percent; community, social, and personal services, 19 percent; government, 13 percent; wholesale and retail trade, 20 percent; construction, 10 percent; transportation and communication, 6 percent; agriculture, forestry, and fishing, 7 percent; utilities, 1 percent.

Holidays: National holidays include New Year's Day (January 1), the Queen's Birthday (April 30), Memorial Day: Liberation of the Netherlands (May 5), and Christmas holidays (December 25 and 26). Religious holidays include Palm Sunday, Good Friday, Holy Saturday, Easter Sunday, Easter Monday, Ascension, Whitmonday, and Christmas Day. Children celebrate St. Nicholas Eve on December 5.

Customs: The Dutch are very friendly to their neighbors and family. Guests are given cheeses or chocolates and pastries. Dutch families spend much of their free time together. Birthdays are special days celebrated with family and friends. The queen's birthday is celebrated with a parade. On St. Nicholas Day children receive their gifts accompanied by special poems. Flower festivals are held each spring.

Culture: Many famous artists come from The Netherlands. Their paintings hang in art museums in Amsterdam and other cities. Today the government helps Dutch artists earn a living. Their works are shown in hospitals, schools, and government buildings. The Concertgebouw Orchestra is one of the world's finest symphony orchestras. Several cities have orchestras. The annual Holland Festival features one month of concerts, operas, ballets, and plays. The Royal Library at the Hague has over one million books. Dutch literature is not very well known outside The Netherlands.

Recreation: Dutch families enjoy reading together in the evenings. On weekends they may go to a movie or ride bicycles to the beach. About 90 percent of Dutch families own television sets. Everyone who owns a TV or radio must pay a license fee each year.

Sports: Soccer is one of the most popular sports. There are hundreds of soccer teams in The Netherlands. Other sports include bicycle riding, gymnastics, volleyball, running, walking marathons, swimming, and sailing. Ice-skating is a popular winter sport. Schools and businesses sometimes close so that people can go ice-skating. Hockey is another popular winter sport. Everyone is encouraged to participate in sports. When the Dutch settled in New Amsterdam they brought the game of Dutch pins, or bowling, with them.

Health: The Netherlands has the world's second highest average life expectancy. Women live to about seventy-nine years. Men live to about seventy-two years. Infant deaths in The Netherlands are among the lowest in the world.

Communications: The Netherlands has over eighty daily newspapers. The Dutch spend about forty-five minutes each day reading the newspaper. The government owns the television and radio networks. Programs for radio and television are made by private independent foundations, too. The government also owns the postal, telegraph, and telephone services.

Transportation: Many people ride bicycles to work. About one half of the people own bicycles. Motor bicycles are also popular. Freight is shipped on 4,000 mi. (6,400 km) of rivers and canals. There are about 28,500 mi. (45,870 km) of roads and over 2,000 mi. (3,200 km) of railroad tracks. Amsterdam and Rotterdam are among the world's busiest seaports. The government partly owns the Royal Dutch Airlines (KLM), one of the world's oldest airlines.

Schools: Almost 95 percent of all Dutch children go to nursery schools, which cover ages four to six. All children must complete ten years of school from ages six to sixteen. Primary education is much like elementary school in the United States. Many children learn English, French, and German. Instead of high school, students attend specialized schools that prepare them for jobs or university studies. There are thirteen universities in The Netherlands. The oldest is the State University of Leiden, founded in 1575. The largest is the University of Amsterdam with twenty thousand students.

Principal Products:
Agriculture: Barley, dairy products, flower bulbs, oats, potatoes, sugar beets, wheat.

Fishing: Mussels, flatfish, herring, haddock, and eels.

Manufacturing: Clothing, electronic equipment, iron, steel, machinery, petroleum products, processed foods, textiles, and transportation equipment.

Mining: Natural gas, petroleum, salt.

IMPORTANT DATES

16,000 B.C.—Prehistoric people arrive on Texel Island

4,000 B.C.—First permanent settlers arrive in The Netherlands

500 B.C.—Frisian, Celtic, Germanic, and other tribes settle in The Netherlands

325 B.C.—Pytheas arrives in The Netherlands

58 B.C.—Julius Caesar conquers The Netherlands

A.D. 28—Frisians murder tax collectors

400-800—Franks rule The Netherlands

870—Netherlands under rule of East Frankish Kingdom

1040—Janskerk built

1048—Pieterskerk built

1100s—Trade and industry increase; The Netherlands increases size by building polders and dikes

1228—About 100,000 persons drown in coastal flood

1240—Dam built on Amstel River

1248—Castle built which later becomes The Hague

1253—St. Martin's destroyed by fire

1280—Knights' Hall built

1287—About 50,000 persons drown in coastal flood

1299—Rotterdam founded

1300—Old Church of St. Nicholas built

1300s-1400s—Dukes of Burgundy rule The Netherlands

1408—New Church built

1421—St. Elizabeth flood

1516—Charles V becomes king of Spain

1568—Eighty Years' War begins

1568—National anthem thought to have been written

1573—Spanish begin siege of Leiden

1574—Siege of Leiden lifted on October 3

1575—University of Leiden founded by William the Silent

1579—Parts of the constitution written

1579—Union of Utrecht formed

1581—Dutch Republic begins; The Netherlands a free and independent country; William the Silent head of the government

1594-1596—Willem Barents explores the far northern seas

1601-1700—The Netherlands becomes a leading world power during its Golden Age

1602—Dutch East India Company formed

1609-1621—Temporary peace between Spain and The Netherlands

1609—Henry Hudson explores New York State for the Dutch

1610—Henry Hudson discovers Hudson Bay in Canada

1612—Beemster Lake becomes Beemster Polder

1615—Willem Schouten discovers Cape Horn in South America

1620s—The Netherlands takes control of part of what is now Indonesia

1621—The Dutch West India Company founded

1624—The Dutch West India Company colonizes New Netherland

1624—Fort Orange built, the first permanent settlement in New Netherland

1625—New Amsterdam founded

1626—The Dutch buy Manhattan Island from the Indians

1630—The modern Dutch flag first used; the Dutch claim part of Brazil

1634—Dutch capture Netherlands Antilles from the Spanish

1642—Abel Tasman discovers New Zealand and Tasmania

1648—Spanish recognize The Netherlands as an independent country

1650s—Dutch Boers settle in South Africa

1652-1674—The Netherlands fights three sea wars against England

1667—The Dutch trade New York State to the English for Surinam

1670—France and England form a secret alliance

1672—France and England attack the Dutch Republic

1674—English and Dutch make peace; hurricane strikes Utrecht and partially wrecks the Dom

1678—French and Dutch make peace

1688-1697 — England and Netherlands fight France

1702-1713 — England and Netherlands fight France

1775 — Netherlands helps Americans fight revolution against England

1780-1784 — Dutch fight Fourth English War

1795-1813 — Netherlands called Batavian Republic under French rule

1795 — French make Amsterdam the capital

1806 — Louis Bonaparte becomes king of Netherlands

1810 — Netherlands made part of France

1813 — Netherlands drives out the French

1814 — The Hague restored as seat of government; constitution written

1815 — The Netherlands and Belgium unite as Kingdom of The Netherlands

1830 — Belgium revolts and becomes an independent country

1870 — New period of growth begins in The Netherlands

1872 — Waterway connects Rotterdam to North Sea, making it an important seaport

1890 — Luxembourg won't accept a female ruler and ends ties with Dutch royal family

1891 — Philips Lamp Company founded

1914-1918 — The Netherlands continues policy of neutrality during World War I

1932 — Zuider Zee dike completed

1940-1945 — Germans occupy The Netherlands during World War II

1940 — Much of Rotterdam destroyed by German bombs

1942 — Japan captures Netherlands East Indies

1945- 1949 — Netherlands East Indies fights to win independence from The Netherlands

1945 — The Netherlands becomes a charter member of the United Nations

1947 — The Netherlands receives aid under the United States' Marshall Plan

1948 — Queen Wilhelmina gives up the throne to her daughter Juliana

1953 — Storm drowns approximately 1,800 people

1954 — Surinam and the Netherlands Antilles become semi-autonomous parts of the Kingdom

1957 — The Netherlands becomes part of the European Common Market

1958 — Delta Plan begins

1962 — United Nations given control of Netherlands New Guinea

1963 — Control of Netherlands New Guinea passes to Indonesia; now called Irian Jaya

1975 — Surinam becomes independent

1975 and 1977 — Moluccan terrorists hold Dutch train passengers hostage

1980 — Queen Beatrix begins her reign

1985 — The Delta Plan scheduled to be completed

IMPORTANT PEOPLE

Adrian VI (1459-1523), pope, born in Utrecht

Tobias Michael Carel Asser (1838-1913), Nobel Peace Prize winner, statesman, and lawyer, born in Amsterdam

Willem Barents (?-1597), navigator, Barents Sea named in his honor, birthplace unknown

Willem Bilderdijk (1756-1831), writer, born in Amsterdam

Herman Boerhaave (1668-1738), doctor, born in Voorhout

Louis Bonaparte (1778-1846), made king of Holland by his brother Napoleon, born in Ajaccio, Corsica

Hieronymus Bosch (1450-1516), painter, born in 's Hertogenbosch

Charlemagne (742-814), Frankish king who converted most of The Netherlands to Christianity, born in Aachen

Charles V (1500-1558), king of Spain who ruled The Netherlands, born in Vincennes

Clovis (466-511), first Frankish king to become a Christian, born in Tournai

Petrus Josephus Wilhelmus Debye (1884-1966), Nobel Prize-winning chemist, born in Maastricht

Eduard Douwes Dekker (1820-1887), writer, pen name Multatuli, born in Amsterdam

Alfons Diepenbrock (1862-1921), composer, born in Amsterdam

Cornelis Dopper (1870-1939), composer, born in Amsterdam

Christian Eijkman (1858-1930), Nobel Prize-winning physiologist, born in Nijkerk

Desiderius Erasmus (1466?-1536), humanist, born in Rotterdam

Anne Frank (1929-1945), author of *The Diary of a Young Girl*, born in Frankfurt, Germany

Wessel Gansfort (1420?-1489), philosopher, born in Groningen

Vincent van Gogh (1853-1890), painter, born in Groot-Zundert

Herman Gorter (1864-1927), writer, born in Wormerveer

Hugo Grotius (1583-1645), statesman, born in Delft

Bernard Haitink (1929-   ), orchestra conductor, born in Amsterdam

Frans Hals (1580?-1666), painter, born in Mechelen

Dirck Hartog (dates unknown), navigator who sailed the Australian coast, birthplace unknown

Meindert Hobbema (1638-1709), painter, born in Amsterdam

Pieter de Hooch (1629-1677), painter, born in Rotterdam

Henry Hudson (?-1611), English navigator who sailed for the Dutch East India Company, birthplace unknown

Christiaan Huygens (1629-1695), scientist who discovered the rings of Saturn, born in The Hague

Constantijn Huygens (1596-1687), poet and father of Christiaan Huygens, born in The Hague

Anton van Leeuwenhoek (1632-1723), scientist who observed microorganisms through microscopes he built, born in Delft

Hendrik Antoon Lorentz (1853-1928), Nobel Prize-winning physicist, born in Arnhem

Willem Mengelberg (1871-1951), orchestra conductor, born in Utrecht

Piet Mondrian (1872-1944), painter, born in Amersfoort

Jacob Obrecht (1453-1505), composer, born in Bergen op Zoom

Heike Kamerlingh Onnes (1853-1926), Nobel Prize-winning physicist, born in Groningen

Philip II (1527-1598), son of Charles V, ruled The Netherlands from 1556 to 1559, born in Valladolid

Willem Pijper (1894-1974), composer, born in Leidschendam

Queen Beatrix (1938-   ), born in Baarn

Queen Juliana (1909-   ), born in The Hague

Queen Wilhemina (1880-1962), born in The Hague

Rembrandt Harmenszoon van Rijn (1606-1669), painter, born in Leiden

Julius Rontgen (1855-1932), composer, born in Leipzig

Jacob van Ruisdael (1628-1682), painter, born in Haarlem

Willem Schouten (1567?-1625), mariner who named Cape Horn for his birthplace, Hoorn

Baruch Spinoza (1632-1677), philosopher, born in Amsterdam

Jan Steen (1626-1669), painter, born in Leiden

Simon Stevinius (1548-1620), mathematician, born in Bruges

Jan Swammerdam (1637-1680), scientist who discovered the red blood corpuscles, born in Amsterdam

Jan Pieterszoon Sweelinck (1562-1621), composer, born in Deventer

Abel Janszoon Tasman (1603-1659), mariner who discovered what is now Tasmania, born in Lutjegast

Eduard van Beinum (1901-1950), orchestra conductor, born in Arnhem

Bernard van Dieren (1884-1936), composer, born in Rotterdam

Jonannesdiderik van der Waals (1837-1923), Nobel Prize-winning scientist who studied gases and liquids, born in Leiden

Joost van den Vondel (1587-1679), writer, born in Cologne, Germany

Jacobus Hendricus van't Hoff (1852-1911), Nobel Prize-winning chemist, born in Rotterdam

Jan Vermeer (1628-1682), painter, born in Haarlem

William the Silent (1533-1585), leader of The Dutch Republic

Frits Zernike (1888-1966), Nobel Prize-winning physicist, born in Amsterdam

INDEX

Page numbers that appear in boldface type indicate illustrations

126

About the Author

Dennis Fradin attended Northwestern University on a partial creative writing scholarship and graduated in 1967. He has published stories and articles in such places as *Ingenue, The Saturday Evening Post, Scholastic, Chicago, Oui,* and *National Humane Review.* His previous books include the Young People's Stories of Our States series for Childrens Press and *Bad Luck Tony* for Prentice-Hall. He is married and the father of three children.